APOLOGIA AND TWO FOLK PLAYS

THE WASHINGTON STRINDBERG
Translations and Introductions by Walter Johnson

Strindberg and the Historical Drama by Walter Johnson

Apologia
and Two Folk Plays

THE GREAT HIGHWAY
THE CROWNBRIDE
SWANWHITE

by AUGUST STRINDBERG

Translations and Introductions
by Walter Johnson

University of Washington Press
Seattle and London

839, 72
5918 a Xe

Library of Congress Cataloging in Publication Data

Strindberg, August, 1849–1912.
  Apologia and two folk plays.

  (*His* The Washington Strindberg)
  Bibliography: p.
  CONTENTS: The great highway.—The crownbride.—
Swanwhite.
    I. Title.
PT9811.A3J56/1981   839.7'26   80-51072
  ISBN 0-295-95760-3

Preface

IN THIS VOLUME are three important members of the Strindberg canon: *The Great Highway* (1909), the last play he wrote; and two folk plays, *The Crownbride* (1901), a major contribution to the neoromantic revival of interest in the folk, and *Swanwhite* (1901), a very personal but not autobiographical folktale in dramatic form. All three are among his forty or so plays which must not be disregarded by anyone who wishes to understand Strindberg's contributions to world drama and theater.

The Great Highway differs from the other two plays in this volume in that it is deliberately and frankly autobiographical and is largely in verse form. Tormented by pangs of conscience about his past and present and irritated by what he considered unjust and malicious criticism from many of his prominent countrymen, he indulged in searching self-scrutiny and came to conclusions that comprise a defense of his behavior on his journey through an imperfect life in an imperfect world. It is a moving defense which emphasizes above all else his regret that he did not become what he would have liked to be: a whole being capable of rising above destructive involvement in the pettiness of the human scene and of serving as a spectator of and interpreter for his fellow human beings.

While very little of *The Crownbride* is in verse form and even these sections are quoted from various sources, the play is essentially poetic in spirit. Although its form resembles that of several of his other plays, its content is an application of ballad and of folktale to a nineteenth-century rural Swedish tragedy. Reminiscent of two of his historical dramas—*Gustav Vasa* (1899) and *Engelbrekt* (1901)—because of its setting (i.e., place) in Dalarna, *The Crownbride* is fascinating for many reasons, not least for its imaginative and faithful presentation of a folk's lifestyle.

Swanwhite is Strindberg's outstanding achievement in presenting what is childlike to those who are children or who have retained the ability to "suspend disbelief" and to enter into the spirit of childlike delight in a fairytale well told. The pleasure of discovering how an author generally concerned with adults and their worlds deals with material usually appealing to the very young in age and/or spirit is one very real reward in this drama.

In translating these plays, I have, as I usually do, relied on the text in the Landquist edition. Convinced that Strindberg knew what he was doing in terms of drama and theater, I have tried to make my translation idiomatically faithful to the originals. I have not tried to "adapt" them.

Walter Johnson

Contents

Illustrations

APOLOGIA AND TWO FOLK PLAYS

Introduction to 'The Great Highway'

IN 1909 STRINDBERG had good reason to contemplate his past, his present, and whatever future he might have. On January 22 he had turned sixty, he was increasingly subject to bodily pain, he had achieved a measure of welcome solitude in the Blue Tower, but had not conquered his inclination to be engaged in debate on matters ranging from the literary to the political. He had a strong feeling that he was being shelved to the benefit of younger rivals in spite of the facts that his Intimate Theater was succeeding and that several of his plays were being presented in other theaters. He was also disturbed by qualms about his own past and not a little enraged about the treatment he believed his fellow human beings had meted out to him.

The drama into which he poured the essence of his contemplation of his own life and of Life in general is *The Great Highway*. This play closely relates to his whole dramatic production in its use of analysis and synthesis. But it is closest to the Damascus trilogy in its deliberate use of synthesis in terms of himself. *The Great Highway* is as autobiographical, subjective, and personal as the trilogy but differs from the three earlier plays in that it is primarily explanatory rather than confessional. It is his defense and justification for his life, *not* an attempt to gain reconciliation with Providence and his fellowmen; it is his "apologia pro vita sua." Admissions are, however, telling and effective parts of the defense.

3

The Great Highway differs from the trilogy, moreover, in its structure: It is a closet drama that does remarkably well in, say, a Readers' Theater or Readers' Workshop. Labeled "A Drama of Wandering with Seven Stations," it consists largely of inner dialog among the various selves of an aging human being looking at his life. Among them are the Wanderer, the Hermit, the Hunter, and even the Tempter. While these are decidedly reminiscent of "characters" in the trilogy, their participation in dramatic action is comparatively slight, and their exploitation of details out of the author's life minor. Predominantly lyrical, the play may be said to be a series of extended reflective lyrics in Strindbergian free verse with some interspersed prose passages.

That Life is difficult is clear to the Wanderer who makes the journey assigned to him, to the Hermit who knows it is wise to withdraw into solitude so as not to become involved, to the Hunter who searches for his Self or soul which he has lost because of his very makeup (he is gregarious, he wants to participate, he wants to play a role), and to the Tempter who questions withdrawal and search and suggests compromise upon compromise for conventionally prized rewards (acceptance, security).

Even the other figures are little more than shadows out of past and present that cause him remorse, need for self-justification, or longing for the realization of inner tranquility. The two millers, Miller A's wife, the photographer and his family, and the organgrinder are all representative of human beings who have wished to exploit him; Klara and the child are representative of what he has lost in life; Möller, the schoolmaster, and the smith represent people he has testified against in ways that torture his conscience; a woman represents his disciples whom he may have led astray; and the Japanese—interestingly named

Hiroshima—is a reminder that it is possible to achieve moral stature in spite of the world and its ways.

Scene 1, the first station or halt in the journey, makes it clear what the Hunter is seeking:

> get back my soul
> my self they have stolen . . .

He has made the journey "upwards and onwards" into the heights of solitude where he can approach the Great Teacher and contemplate nature in all its glory. Searching for his soul while escaping from human bonds (friendship, generosity, fellowship, love, beauty, exploiters, and the like), he is tempted into returning to the world with its "warm breath of living people" in spite of the fact that he knows he can not refrain from taking part in human activities and in spite of the sensible advice another of his selves, the Wanderer, gives him:

> One travels best Incognito, and believe me
> one should always become acquainted
> but never get to know,
> one doesn't, of course,
> one just thinks one does . . . So:
> in company, without friendship, without enmity . . .

Scene 2, the second halt, deals not only with inevitable involvement but self-assessment, too. The dialog between the doubles, the Wanderer (Incognito) and the Hunter (the searcher for identity), plays with one of Strindberg's favorite convictions—that human beings are by nature vampires to some degree and involve themselves and each other no matter how much any individual may try to remain a spectator. It makes clear, too, that the sensitive Wanderer needs artificial protection—wine to serve as a drug and clothes to serve as concealment or cover up.

Even the poet as Wanderer with poetic insight ("the skill of being able to read people") finds his arrogant self-assessment wrong. "Life, experience, certain books, an inborn superior intelligence, and a good portion of acquired sharpsightedness" do not permit him to know others or himself:

> and we are foreigners, remain so to each other.
> We all travel Incognito
> and incognito
> to ourselves!

In Scene 3, the halt in the Village of Jackasses, Strindberg emphasizes the impossibility of talking *with* many if not all people in the sense of actually communicating with them. But the scene is essentially an attack on enemies, who, he alleges, had been foolish or stupid enough to write a silly play and a volume glorifying the king who had ruined his country—two asses who had done stupid things but had been undeservedly rewarded while the deserving poet had not been. Strindberg's sensitivity to slights and injustice has been well documented by himself and others, of course, but his stooping to bitter attack on rivals whom he considered inferiors and even fools is an admission of personal flaws, of course, even though at the time of writing he had the conviction he was more than justified in his attacks.

The fourth scene, the arcade in the poet's native city, is Strindberg's synthetic account of his return home to a city in which the people have rejected Christianity for faith in the theory of evolution, a city in which people are robbers spying on each other or, if you will, denigrators, defamers, vampires. It is, moreover, a city with its memories of brief moments of happiness, of people he has loved but who no longer exist as they did. It is a city that does not dare prosecute the psychic murderer and corrupter Möller, that does not distribute rewards justly, that does not recognize the worth of a human being with integrity (the Japanese), and that has not benefited from the poet's confession of his own sins or from his confession of the sins of others:

> HUNTER: Yes!—Twelve years ago I committed hara-kiri; I executed my old self, and the one you see here you do not know, can never get to know!
>
> MURDERER: Yes, I remember you were stupid enough . . . to get up on the pillory to confess publicly, on the scarlet carpet, all your faults and weaknesses . . .
>
> HUNTER: And the whole community enjoyed it, all of them felt they were better people, and thought themselves made righteous through my public, civil death. They had neither a word of sympathy nor approval for my confession of sins.
>
> MURDERER: Why should they have had?
>
> HUNTER: After ten years of suffering when I had set things right, it occurred to me that I ought to confess your sins, too! Then there was another tune. . . .

His confession of personal "faults and weaknesses" had been put into black and white in his post-Inferno autobiographies and particularly in the Damascus trilogy; his confession of others' sins, into his post-Damascus dramas of testimony and his post-Damascus prose fiction.

The fifth halt contains not only the most telling parts of Strindberg's assessment of life itself but his justification for his cruel and brutal psychic murder of Gustaf af Geijerstam, in *Black Banners* (*Svarta fanor*):

> When I stripped you, you died!
> Worshipper of idols! That was your name,
> your character! You forced one to adore
> your horrid mate and your detestable sons;
> one had to, or else one was sacrificed
> and cut up with a knife every Saturday,

and lynched besides in the Sunday number—
robbed of bread and honor!

Obscure as the details of the stripping may be, it should be
clear enough to the reader that Strindberg's conscience was
disturbed by memories of what he had done to a fellow
· human being.

While much of Scene 5 is devoted to what people do to
each other, the assessment of life itself—in the dialog
between the Hunter and the Japanese and given in a series of
reflective lyrics—is crucial to what Strindberg was trying to
do in *The Great Highway*:

> But all that is as nothing though,
> nothing compared to the fact of life itself—
> the humility of wandering
> a bare skeleton clothed in flesh,
> and set going with sinews, cords,
> by a tiny motor in the chest's
> engine room, propelled by the heat
> the stomach's furnace can get up—
> and the soul, the spirit sits in the heart
> like a bird in the cage of one's breast,
> a basket or a net.

Having to take the great comedy of life seriously, having to
consider sacred what is coarse, learning that beauty and the
ideal do not really exist on Earth, and having to regret the
good one has done: all these mar the journey, the wandering
through life.

The sixth halt or scene ("At the last gate") is a poetic
interpretation of family and home, the best life has to offer,
and what he had done with them in the "madhouse, . . .
prison, . . . house of correction" the world is:

> For there is happiness, no doubt of that,
> but brief, as the flash of lightning,

as sunshine, as the morning glory—
one blossom and *one* day,
and then the end!

Now in his old age as he sees it, the poet sees "everything, everything" and that fact is the source of very little comfort. He has "lost" even the youngest of his children, a little innocent who does not know he is her father.

The last scene or halt, "The dark forest," is Strindberg's final evaluation in lyric and dramatic form of human beings and the lives they lead as well as of himself and the life he has led. In the rich potential of reflective lyric form rather than in the cold analytic form of a case report, he concludes:

Bless me, bless your humanity,
which suffers, suffers from the gift of Life!
Me first, who has suffered most—
who has suffered most from the agony
of being unable to be what I wanted to be!

It is a remarkably revealing and persuasive plea!

As the brief comments on the content have suggested, Strindberg's apologia deals, on the one hand, with deity and the world that deity has created (earth, life and afterlife, human beings, human relations) and, on the other, with the poet and the life he has led (his nature, his dream, his roles, his experiences, his judgment of the gifts of life, his final hope).

The Great Teacher, the Only True One, the poet suggests, is revealed in His creation as well as in written revelations:

Nature's silent when the Great Teacher speaks!
Look!—A flash of lightning from east to west—
He writes His name with ink of fire,
on a coal black cloud! I know You,

eternal, invisible one, yet seen,
stern, ever compassionate!

Just as in many a reflective lyric, Strindberg's treatment of deity is a matter of suggestion, *not* of analysis. Yet the suggestions are more than adequate in revealing the poet's basic faith in God as the Creator, the Disciplinarian, the Redeemer, and the Provider of more than merely transitory hope—an afterlife conceived of by the poet as an infinite improvement over this life.

"The agony of being unable to be what I wanted to be" is surely the key statement in his defense. Again and again Strindberg makes it clear that he had wanted to be without flaws, that he was an idealist, and, distressingly in a human context what is futile, a perfectionist.

For the poet, Life has been a gift, which has proved humiliating ("a skeleton clothed in flesh"); his life has been a journey, a wandering without signposts a human being *can* be guided by; life has proved a constant struggle between looking on and taking part in the human (tragi-) comedy. Like other human beings, he has become a sinner in a society of sinners, but, unlike some, a thinking, feeling, guilt-ridden sinner, who hates being what people are—highwaymen, outlaws.

He is well aware of his failure to attain what he wanted to be. Note his laments over becoming involved (in a war of words, for example), over being exploited by others (by the photographer and his family, for example), over being treated unjustly (by those to whom he has been generous, for example), and over his own failures (his gullibility, his arrogance, his pretensions). But he has tried, not altogether unsuccessfully as the various roles he says he has had suggest: architect, soldier, preacher, witness, wanderer, hermit, hunter, questioner, and penitent and, one should add, husband, parent, citizen, friend, enemy, observer, "observed," and gregarious human being. In a manner reminiscent of his *The Secret of the Guild* (1882), he has planned and built houses, including *the* theater in his native city: that role has obviously to do with his creative writing as well. As a soldier, he has fought for what he has considered good; as a preacher and a witness, he has tried to promote what is right; and as a wanderer, hermit, hunter, and questioner, he has tried to come to terms with life, his fellow human beings, and God.

As a penitent, he has confessed his sins (in his dramas and novels of confession) and has testified about other people's sins (in his dramas and novels of testimony):

> MURDERER: Yes, I remember you were stupid enough . . . to get up on the pillory to confess publicly, on the scarlet carpet, all your faults and weaknesses . . .
>
> HUNTER: After ten years of suffering when I had set things right, it occurred to me that I ought to confess your sins, too!

His penitence is not complete but is a blend of self-justification and remorse, though not when he sees the urn containing the ashes of the man (Gustaf af Geijerstam) he had psychically murdered (in *Black Banners*). In none of his many roles has he been able to gain the inner tranquility and peace he has been seeking. Proven false too is his arrogant assumption that because of his superior endowment, book knowledge, special life-experiences, and acquired insight he can "read," that is, see into and understand people.

Even though *The Great Highway* may never serve conventional theaters as a superb play for production, its merits are such that it should not be overlooked or disregarded. Because it is Strindberg's last statement in dramatic form, it is extremely important for the student of

Strindberg as autobiographer, for the reader who wishes to gain an understanding of Strindberg the lyricist at his best, for any reader who finds delight in a master's use of imagery and symbol, and for any person who may well find in Strindberg's apologia striking similarities to his own assessments of Life, which goes on generation after generation, and life, which is the gift meted out briefly to each human being.

The Great Highway[1]

A Drama of Wandering
with
Seven Stations

'Characters'

THE HUNTER

THE HERMIT

THE WANDERER

MILLER A

MILLER E

MILLER A'S WIFE

THE GIRL

THE SCHOOLMASTER

THE SMITH

THE ORGANGRINDER

THE PHOTOGRAPHER

THE PHOTOGRAPHER'S WIFE
(EUPHROSYNE)

GOTTHARD, *their son*

KLARA, *the girl in the flower shop, the Hunter's daughter*

THE JAPANESE

THE MURDERER (*Möller*)

THE CHILD, *the Hunter's daughter* (*Maria*)

A VOICE

A WOMAN

THE TEMPTER

PEOPLE (*a few*)

Settings

1. On the Alps
2. By the windmills
3. In Eselsdorf (the Village of Jackasses)
4. An arcade in the city
5. In the park outside the crematory
6. At the last gate
7. The dark forest

The music in "the dark forest" is Chopin's Nocturne 13, op. 48 no. 1, and this is played softly in the distance until the end of the play.

I

ON THE ALPS

A roadsign with two arms: one upward, one downward.
The background shows dark thunderheads. Later the storm
breaks.

HUNTER (*enters, studies the roadsign*):
Where have I come?—how far?
Well, there the road goes up, down over there!
I can always go down, I want to go up.
But the arms on this sign point
as if warning against the road up!
There's danger then, many dangers
on the path, which is steep and narrow!
That doesn't frighten me—I love danger.
But first I want to rest a little
and catch my breath!
And think, pull myself together,
and get back my self
my self they have stolen . . .

*

I was among people all too long
and lost my soul,
my heart, my thoughts;
they took the rest, they stole—
they bound me with friendliness,
with gifts I didn't ask for;
yes, it was warm down there
going from home to home, by lovely tables,
music and flowers, candles, glasses.

15

But it became hot and stifling—
Then I cut off the mooring
and threw away my ballast, all my burdens,
no matter how dear—and see, I rose!
Here I can breathe, and my heart
and lungs have air again;
neither dust, nor smoke, nor people's breath
poisons my blood.
                          Pure, white snow
of sublimated vapor. Water diamonds,
lilies turned to stone by cold,
the flour of heaven sifted through the dark
sieve of clouds—
holy silence, draw your silky cover
over the head of this weary wanderer,
who goes to bed and whispers forth his prayer.
                          *

What's that up north? A cliff of slate,
a cloud just like the blackboard in school,
still blank—what's that? The teacher's coming.
And the class gets silent.
Nature's silent when the Great Teacher speaks!
Look!—A flash of lightning from east to west—
He writes His name with ink of fire
on a coal black cloud! I know You,
eternal, invisible one, yet seen,
stern, ever compassionate!—
The mountain pines bend low
and the brooks stand silent, still.
The frightened goat falls to his knees,
his head bared the vulture crouches,
on the Alp's ridge; Nature trembles!—
I'm called lord of creation,
a mockery for which I'm not to blame,

I bend low in shame,
meanest of all before the throne of Your omnipotence.

*

Look, the cloud is rent! The curtain drawn
to the sides! What do I see?
Fair earth! Temptress,
that draws me back down—
How lovely you are!
In the green of hope and the blue of faithfulness,
the rose-red of love.
The tall pines painted by the sunset,
the cypress trees by grave and night,
a cliff with a marble temple,
if it's honor's or happiness' we'll see,
a grotto, home of a gray sibyl,
who frightens the nymphs in the olive grove—

Now comes the sun! How it glistens
from the rose-red stones of frost; the clouds edged
with silver bands, the pitch-black hoods
hung in the attic to be aired!
What's moving? Who hides the sun?
And draws shadows on the white snow?
A royal eagle, *chrysaëtos*,[2] golden on his breast.
Knight of the air in golden byrnie
and knightly chain about your throat—

What? You're sinking? Going down into the valley
when your wings tire, your tail's rudder
can't steer the upward course?
Yes, he wants to descend! Down! Down to rest,
and breathe the warm breath of living people,
and smell the fragrance from the clover—
why, it's summer down there still. . . .

There the water in the clouds drops like pearls;
here like brilliants, diamonds;
there the brook murmurs, here it's struck silent,
here lonely fields of snow, though with white flowers—
down there white daisies . . .
Up here and down there! Here and there,
one's driven, to just as good and just as bad!

*

HERMIT: Whither? *Quo vadis,*[3] Wanderer?
You've come halfway and are looking back.
But *Excelsior*[4] was your watchword up to now!
HUNTER:
    It still is!
HERMIT: What are you seeking up here?
HUNTER: My self, which I lost down there!
HERMIT: What you lost down there
    you can surely not find again up here?
HUNTER: You're so right! But if I go down there I'll lose still
    more, and never find what I lack.
HERMIT: You're really afraid for your skin . . .
HUNTER: Not my skin, but for my soul . . .
HERMIT: You don't love human beings . . .
HUNTER: Yes, much too much, that's why I fear them . . .
HERMIT: To love is to give—give!
HUNTER: They don't want to receive, but take;
    They don't take the gift alone but the giver, too!
HERMIT: But the Shepherd gave Himself for the flock . . .
HUNTER: Well, dust returns to dust, but the spirit belongs to
    God.
HERMIT: You're good at fencing with your tongue, you ought
    to use the pen!
At any rate, your life is half over;
don't abort the fetus, too early birth
can never make you a man, a human being;

live out your life, go down again, it's not dangerous;
if there's dust on the highway, brush it off;
there are ditches on the sides; fall into them.
But get up. There are gates,
jump over, creep under, unlatch the hook;
you'll meet people; embrace them,
they don't bite, but if they do, the bite isn't dangerous,
if you're soaked, let it run off.
Spend your coin, you'll get it back,
there's nothing to win up here,
for stone is stone, and snow is snow—
but human beings—they're something else.
HUNTER: I know they are, if only I could
remain a spectator and sit in the audience,
but I want to get up on stage, to act, to play along;
but when I take a role, I'm lost,
and forget who I am . . .
HERMIT: Who are you?
HUNTER: Nice! Now we'll stop . . .
It'll really be too cold for me up here.
HERMIT: And the air's a bit thin, and all too lonely . . .
Watch it, here's company!
HUNTER: A strange fellow! Comes from up above,
looks a bit all in; stand still, Wanderer!

*

WANDERER: I come from the brow of the cliff,
have bathed in air, but don't stay in the bath;
one gets dressed, of course, and wanders on,
with a companion or without, preferably with!
What's the name of the land over there, Hermit?
HERMIT: The land of wishes!
WANDERER: The land of pious wishes?
HERMIT: Pious or wild
according to . . .

WANDERER: what they're for!
Oh well! I see I'll get company here!
With whom do I have the honor?
HUNTER: I'm a soldier.
WANDERER: And I'm a wanderer.
One travels best Incognito, and believe me
one should always become acquainted
but never get to know,
one doesn't, of course,
one just thinks one does . . . So:
in company, without friendship, without enmity,
two steps apart, not too close,
forward! And downward, then the even road.
Up one hill, down one hill.
A tavern, a stop, a little glass,
but keep the course straight south!
HUNTER: With the sun as beacon we'll not get lost,
it doesn't go out, and the keeper never falls asleep . . .
I think he's left us, our Hermit?
WANDERER: Yes, let him go! It doesn't matter,
not down there where we're going!
He has made his choice and said farewell to the world!
HUNTER: Perhaps he's right.
WANDERER: Don't look up there!
For "worldly vainly" rhyme as "hither, thither,"
but we're not going over there, but . . . over here!

[CURTAIN]

2

BY THE WINDMILLS

The background a cloudy sky. To the sides two windmills, called Adam and Eve, one on each side and a tavern to the right. The WANDERER *and the* HUNTER *are at a table, each with a glass.*

WANDERER: It's quiet down here in the valley.

HUNTER: A little too quiet, the miller thinks,

WANDERER: who's sleeping, no matter how much water's running;

HUNTER: since he functions by weather and wind . . .

WANDERER: which pointless activity has aroused a certain aversion to windmills in me.

HUNTER: Just as in the noble knight Don Quixote of La Mancha,[5]

WANDERER: who didn't turn his coat by the wind,

HUNTER: but rather the opposite;

WANDERER: for which he even got into trouble. Are we sitting here playing that game?

HUNTER: Mr. Incognito, why are you drinking so much?

WANDERER: Since I'm always lying on the operating table, I chloroform myself!

HUNTER: Then we won't ask any more questions.

WANDERER: I've probably said too much!

HUNTER: Imagine, I can't guess what you are.

WANDERER: Quit guessing; that's much more pleasant.

HUNTER: Actually, yes!—It's cloudy all day today.

WANDERER: Let me empty this a bit, and you'll see it'll ease up! (*Drinks*) Do you know Greek? Do you know what *oinos* means?

HUNTER: *Oinos* means wine.

WANDERER: Yes, wine! So you have been a student?

HUNTER: *Noli me tangere!* Don't touch me! I sting!

WANDERER: Have you noticed the grape looks like a bottle, and the tendril like a corkscrew? That's a definite signature.

HUNTER: But the juice has none of the qualities of chloroform,

WANDERER: before the berries have been crushed under foot and rotted into scum and dregs;

HUNTER: so that the spirit of the wine has been set free from the filthy cover of matter,

WANDERER: and rises to the surface like foam on the sea,

HUNTER: from which Aphrodite[6] was born,

WANDERER: naked

HUNTER: without even a vineleaf to cover her,

WANDERER: because clothes are merely the consequence of the fall through sin.[7]—Are you always this serious?

HUNTER: Are you always this facetious?

WANDERER: Which of us two is most inquisitive?

HUNTER: Now you're stretching out your tentacles to catch me . . .

WANDERER: subject to the law of universal attraction,

HUNTER: which is accompanied by mutual repulsion,

WANDERER: which makes it best to keep two steps apart and march on in single file . . .

HUNTER: according to the agreement as of this date. Period. Here come the actors!

*

WANDERER: May I borrow your glasses? My eyesight's a bit weak.

*

WANDERER: What do I see on them? It looks like hoarfrost, crystalized water, or salt;
a tear, dried, warm at its source,
it chilled so quickly, turned to salt;

and the steel of the bows has rusted.
You often weep but in secret,
and the streams of tears have dug their channels
from the eyes down to your mouth,
to turn off the smiles, which would lead to laughter.
Poor human being!
Your mask is worn,
and when you show your teeth,
one doesn't know if it's to bite or smile.

HUNTER: Now the game begins! An idyll with windmills,
WANDERER: a pastoral in minor-major; keep your eyes open
now.

*

MILLER A: Well, neighbor, we're in the same boat today, since
there's no wind at all; but I'm thinking of getting your mill
moved, for you hurt my business.

MILLER E: You mean I rob you of the east wind, but since you
rob me of the west wind it's a toss-up.

MILLER A: But my mill was here first, and you built yours out
of spite. Since it's going badly for both of us, it surely
would be better if it went well for *one* of us.

MILLER E: You mean for you?

MILLER A: You mean for you?

MILLER E: Yes, of course!

MILLER A: But I meant *one* of us, the most deserving, the one
who has right on his side.

MILLER E: Who would that be?

MILLER A: Are we the ones to decide that?

MILLER E: My sieve's better than yours, and my Eve grinds
more quickly, turns more easily, and has new sails.

MILLER A: But my Adam was built before yours, my hopper is
made of boxwood . . .

MILLER E: Hold it! We'll ask the men who are sitting over
there.

*

WANDERER: There, you see! Now we'll get involved.

HUNTER: They want to steal us as witnesses and probably as judges, so they can sit in judgment over our judgment afterwards!

*

MILLER A'S WIFE: Come in for dinner, dear!

MILLER A: Wait a little!

MILLER A'S WIFE: I can't!

MILLER A: You should learn never to be in a hurry.

MILLER A'S WIFE: Never?

MILLER A: Never, as long as the world's still here, and one word will do.

MILLER A'S WIFE: But then the cabbage will get cold.

MILLER A: Are we having cabbage? That's something else! I'll be right in.

MILLER A'S WIFE: But then the world will end, and one word won't do any more.

MILLER A: Did I say that? Then I take it back!

(*They go.*)

*

WANDERER: He sold his birthright,[8]

HUNTER: for a mess of cabbage,

WANDERER: and how good it was.

HUNTER: But now we'll get the Eve-miller at us; see how he has his eye on us—he wants something of us, a bit of information to give direction to what he knows; see now he's looking down . . . he's searching us with his eyes, examining our clothes, shoes, hair, and beards; he's a thief!

*

MILLER E: Excuse me!

WANDERER: He wants to fool us into talking!—Don't answer him!

MILLER E: Where do you gentlemen come from?

WANDERER: That doesn't concern you!

MILLER E: Strictly speaking, no!

WANDERER: Now we'll make it very strict, so go away.

MILLER E: I'm not thinking of taking anything . . .

WANDERER: That wouldn't be so easy either . . .

MILLER E: But I'm thinking of giving you something . . .

WANDERER: We don't need anything!

MILLER E: That's really something!—Well, I was thinking of giving you gentlemen something, and wouldn't charge anything for it—a bit of information! A precious bit of information! (*Pause*) Namely: they're just about to blow up rock just in back—(*Pause*)—and one, two, three we'll have a shower of rocks over our heads. (*The* HUNTER *and the* WANDERER *stand up.*)

WANDERER: Why didn't you say that right off?

MILLER E: Why, you didn't want to listen! But sit down, there's no hurry, for the dynamiters will call out a warning first.

WANDERER: Listen, is this the road to the Promised Land?

MILLER E: This is the direct road . . .

WANDERER: Will there be good weather this afternoon . . . ?

MILLER E: We can expect more thundershowers; it's very unstable in this area.

WANDERER: Is it like that all year?

MILLER E: Always unstable, all year, year in and year out.

WANDERER: And the name of the next town?

MILLER E: That doesn't concern you! It's certainly more pleasant to give than to receive, but to be robbed isn't pleasant. Thief!—Do you have passports?

WANDERER: What do we need those for?

MILLER E: Well, there are robbers in the forest, and all those who don't want to say where they come from, we have to search.

*

HUNTER: There you are! Now we're involved!

WANDERER: In something that doesn't look like a mill idyll.

MILLER E: Now I'll fetch my neighbor and his hired man, so we can quickly check your alibi . . .

WANDERER: That's a strange way . . .

MILLER E: Yes, for I'm a police assistant and so's my neighbor . . . (*Goes*)

WANDERER: And now they've become friends, Herod and Pilate![9]

HUNTER: I had actually set out to keep my self; but the one who wants to keep, must lose. So we throw ourselves into the crowd again . . .

WANDERER: with the risk we'll sink,

HUNTER: without going to the bottom,

WANDERER: thanks to a certain lifebuoy which sensible people always have on their person.—There's a woman,
    (*The* GIRL *enters*)

HUNTER: whom one could expect in the neighborhood of Adam and Eve,

WANDERER: without exactly expecting a paradise.

HUNTER: Period! Now it starts!

*

WANDERER: I think the offensive is more promising . . . What's your name, lovely child?

GIRL: Guess!

WANDERER: Let me see!—Blond, a miller's daughter, rather tiny, a round face—your name is Amalia!

GIRL: How did you know?

WANDERER: I could tell by looking at you!

GIRL: If I were dark, tall, and had an oval face what would have been my name as a smith's daughter?

WANDERER: Jenny, of course!

GIRL: That's right!

WANDERER: Now that you've learned something from me, what do I get for it?

GIRL: You may . . . tell me where you got the skill of being able to read people.

WANDERER: Life, experience, certain books, an inborn superior intelligence, and a good portion of acquired sharpsightedness . . . Tell me: why don't you want the son of the miller next door?

GIRL: So you knew that, too!

WANDERER: But you should take him; then the mill problem would be solved without a lawsuit—you can sell the one mill and have it moved to the next parish where it's needed.

GIRL: How wise, how very wise you are . . .

WANDERER: But I can tell you don't want the miller's boy; I suspect you'd almost rather have one of the robbers in the forest, eh? The one with the dark eyes and the big moustache . . .

GIRL: I'm getting frightened . . . Are you a fortune teller?

WANDERER: As you can hear; but I can tell the fortunes only of young people.

GIRL: How come?

WANDERER: Old people are so sly.

GIRL (*to the* HUNTER): Is all that true?

WANDERER: Don't talk to him, he doesn't want to get involved! Talk to me! Give me something for everything you've learned in this short while—otherwise, you'll be in my debt, and you don't want that!

GIRL: Yes, you'll get something so you won't leave unrewarded, richer than when you came, burdened with truths I won't take anything for . . .

WANDERER: That's a whopper!

GIRL: In the first place, my name isn't Amalia—

WANDERER: but Jenny as I said?

GIRL: No, not that either! In the second place, there isn't any miller's son. In the third, the next parish has four mills so the mill problem will remain unsolved. Further, in addition, you'll get one or two good pieces of advice. Never address an unknown girl by her first name; you can never know whom you're talking with, no matter how sharpsighted you think you are. Further, never be unfaithful to a friend when a third person comes along, because when you're alone again and need him, maybe he won't be there.

WANDERER: I have not been unfaithful!

GIRL: Well, you wanted to poke fun at him just now to play up to me—that wasn't nice.—Now you're on the defensive—and if you asked me now what my name is, I wouldn't answer you the way you answered the miller when he wanted to save you from the robbers in the forest . . .

HUNTER (*gets up*): Won't you sit down, milady?

GIRL: Yes, I'm a lady, from the manor house, and not a miller's daughter . . . (*To the* WANDERER) Go to the miller and greet him from me, and you'll get your passport; just go, and simply greet him from the young lady . . .

WANDERER: But I must know your name!

GIRL (*sits down*): I don't give my name to strangers, and if you're decent, you won't ask for it! Out there!

(*The* WANDERER *goes.*) (*Pause.*)

GIRL: You are lucky, you who can wander, and meet people, get to know many of them . . .

HUNTER: Well, get to know?

GIRL: True! One doesn't!
But get acquainted . . .

HUNTER: Hardly that; guessing
is one way of killing time!

GIRL: For what's
said isn't worth much!
HUNTER: Still!
It has to be translated;
for all languages can be called foreign,
and we are foreigners, remain so to each other.
We all travel Incognito
GIRL: and incognito to
ourselves!
You're in mourning, but you're not dressed in mourning,
HUNTER: and you're dressed like a miller's daughter but are a
lady!
GIRL: And your companion?
HUNTER: Merely an acquaintance,
but a stranger through and through.
GIRL: What do you suspect about that man?
HUNTER: Everything
and nothing!
I haven't summed him up yet!
GIRL: What were you doing up there?
HUNTER: Breathing and
forgetting!
GIRL: But why forget? Without memories our life would be
an empty nothing . . .
HUNTER: and *with* a load on deck that would sink the ship!
GIRL: An unloaded ship goes over most easily . . .
HUNTER: and that's why they usually take on ballast . . .
GIRL: and shorten the sails
HUNTER: as on the windmill,
GIRL: for otherwise its wings may be broken . . .
HUNTER: but he turns best on the heights . . .
GIRL: but best of all in the valleys on the plains . . .
HUNTER: where the air is so condensed,

GIRL: . . . one can see
   for miles,
can count parish churches with the naked eye,
and all the stars of night show up . . .
HUNTER: not on the horizon,
GIRL: but surely in the zenith,
   and you have zenith everywhere, when you've
really reached the horizon . . .
HUNTER: Tell me, when did I
   reach it?
GIRL:: You're sitting in the place, to which you aimed
   to go this morning! Isn't it delightful,
to find something new, when you've really won the old?
HUNTER: But the land in the distance?
GIRL: Go and you'll get
   there . . .
But if you weary, it will draw back!—
No mortal has had the polar star[10] at zenith,
but still they go, and turn back,
and others go the same way, and are driven back.
Do as they! But learn on the way.
HUNTER: One drags, one dredges, one's nose down at
   nadir . . .
GIRL: With one's eyes now and then in the zenith!
   (*Signals on a horn can be heard.*)
HUNTER (*listens intently*):   Listen!
GIRL: I hear it, but I don't understand!
HUNTER: I'll translate!
   You hear only sounds, but I hear words!
GIRL: What does the horn say?
HUNTER: "Answer me: Where are you,
   where?"
   (*The horn answers: "Here!"*)
GIRL: It's someone calling you! (*A new signal*)

HUNTER: "Come this way, come this way, come this way!
This way!"
GIRL: I hear you are a soldier or rather see it!
They're calling you; we part as quickly as we met!
HUNTER: Not quite so quickly, not quite so easily . . .
Come with me a bit on my way
to the next village!
GIRL: And your companion?
HUNTER: I can find the likes of him in any tavern!
GIRL: How cruel you are!
HUNTER: I have declared war!
So it's forward! not standing still!
GIRL: That's why I'm going; otherwise I'll stay!
HUNTER: And if you go, you'll take something along.
GIRL: And if I stay, you'll have taken something from me!
HUNTER (*looking ahead*):
Look! They're quarreling! In a minute they'll be fighting—
They are fighting! And I'll be called to testify!
But you should go; you mustn't be involved.
GIRL: So you're thinking of me?
HUNTER: Of you, for you,
with you and through! Now farewell!
A flower seen through the garden fence,
which delights the wanderer for a moment,
loveliest unbroken, sends only its fragrance
with the wind, for a second, and all's over!
So forward!
GIRL: Farewell! and so forward! (*Goes*)
HUNTER: Now I'm down! Bound, trapped,
drawn into the mill of justice,
with the net of feelings on lovely wings,
allied with a stranger and interested
in a matter that doesn't concern me!

WANDERER [*enters*]: Are you still here? I thought you had left; you must be a faithful soul.

HUNTER: Did you get into a fight?

WANDERER: I hit the miller on his mouth because he had pulled my leg. What he said about dynamiting and robbers in the forest was all lies. We're summoned to the fall session of court, I as defendant in the fight, you as witness.

HUNTER: Did you give them our names?

WANDERER: No, I made up two names on the spur of the moment.

HUNTER: How did you dare? Why, we can get into still another case for falsification . . . To go involving me in this way!—What did you say my name was?

WANDERER: I said you were traveling under the name Incognito! And that really got to the farmers!

HUNTER: And I'm to testify against you?

WANDERER: In three months, yes! So let's use our freedom and march on.—They say there's a festival in the next village!

HUNTER: What kind of festival?

WANDERER: A kind of *jeux floraux*,[11] a festival of jackasses, in which the stupidest fool in town is crowned with a gold crown of paper . . .

HUNTER: That's priceless! What's the name of the town?

WANDERER: Eselsdorf, the Village of Jackasses! But the one we're in is called Lügenwald or Forest of Lies, because only liars live here.

HUNTER: *Enthevten exelavnein*,[12] after that they marched on,

WANDERER: *parasangas treis*, three miles,

HUNTER: and so they did!

[CURTAIN]

3

IN THE VILLAGE OF JACKASSES

Eselsdorf. To the left a smithy; to the right in the background a bench on which the HUNTER *and the* WANDERER *are sitting out of the limelight.*

HUNTER: Now we've been wandering quite a ways together,

WANDERER: and not come a bit closer; not even so I can guess who you are.

HUNTER: I'm a soldier, as I told you; I'm always fighting, you see, fighting to keep my personal independence . . .

WANDERER: But don't always succeed.

HUNTER: One can't expect to,

WANDERER: especially, since the defeats are the most instructive,

HUNTER: for the victor,

WANDERER: but the worst is that one doesn't always know who won; in the latest war the victor lost most.

HUNTER: What war?

WANDERER: At the windmills!

HUNTER: May I borrow your penknife?—I lost mine up in the mountains.

WANDERER: Let's not be inquisitive!—You see, if you look at this knife, it will tell you quite a lot. The big blade is almost unused—so the owner isn't a craftsman; the small blade, on the other hand, shows traces of lead and colored crayons; so he *may* be an artist but could be merely an amateur; the corkscrew is in pretty bad shape—we understand what that means, the porter opener, too! But then there's a drill and a saw! Ta, and there you have a skeleton key—that really tells us something even though it was only thrown in. So: there we didn't get any information!

HUNTER: So! . . . This is Eselsdorf! And there comes the schoolmaster; this time we're going to keep still so we don't get involved.

WANDERER: If that can help!

SCHOOLMASTER (*enters*): Abracadabra, abracadabra— ab-ra-ca-dab-ra! (*Looks at the strangers*) Nah! They didn't hear!—Once more!—Abracadabra; abra-cadabra, abra-ca-da-bra!—Nah! They're civilized people; they have self-control!—Gentlemen, the one who says nothing agrees; now I ask if you'll receive a deputation of the most outstanding intellectuals in the village who will challenge you to a combat of words. If I don't get an answer, I'll assume you consent! One, two, three!

HUNTER AND WANDERER: No!

SCHOOLMASTER: Fine!

WANDERER: You're not so stupid considering you're from Eselsdorf.

SCHOOLMASTER: I'm the only sane man in town, so I have to act crazy; otherwise they'd lock me up! I'm academically trained, I've written a tragedy in five acts in verse called *Potamogeton*;[13] it's so damn stupid I ought to have got the award, but the village smith outflanked me by submitting a memoir about the destroyer[14] of our country, so I was passed over. I'm an unjustly treated victim! You undoubtedly think I'm egotistic because I talk about myself, but there are two reasons for that—firstly, I have to introduce myself, secondly, you don't like to have me talk about you!—Here comes the village smith, so I'll disguise myself, or he'll think I'm sane, and then he'll lock me up. (*He puts on jackass ears.*)

SMITH (*enters*): Abra-ca-da-bra, abra-cadabra!

SCHOOLMASTER: Hello, axe handle!

SMITH: Is that supposed to be a dig at me?

SCHOOLMASTER: Life is a struggle, and we struggle with it!

SMITH: Do you mean that liberation question or free trade?
SCHOOLMASTER: Two times two makes four and six added to that makes eight. Right?
SMITH: I reserve all arithmetic to myself for it is my major field, next to *quatuor species*, which signifies the four rules of arithmetic in integers, including fractions, except ordinary fractions and decimals.
SCHOOLMASTER: At times even Homer nods . . .
SMITH: But six and four make eleven, and if one moves the point two places to the left, it gets even as a nail. Isn't that right, gentlemen? Isn't that right?
WANDERER: Absolutely right; six and four makes eleven, and not eight!
SMITH: Now we'll take the easier component parts, or let me put it: topics of conversation. Gentlemen, a topic of conversation is not blown out of the nose if I may put it like that, even supposing the topic of conversation is light. A light topic of conversation upon closer examination breaks into two equal major parts; first, there is the topic, there should be a topic for everything, and then the conversation follows of itself. The topics again can be as many as . . . as the days in the year, or still more; let's say: the drops in the sea, or still more; as let's say: as the sands in the desert, I haven't ever been in a desert, of course, but I can really imagine how it looks; on the other hand, I did take a trip on a steamship once, it was expensive, gentlemen, assuming that you have never taken such a trip, but that wasn't what I wanted to say! . . .
SCHOOLMASTER: The Guano Islands[15] lie fifty-six degrees North and thirteen degrees East to East to South.
SMITH: Was that supposed to be a dig at me? I don't like digs . . .
SCHOOLMASTER: But still that wasn't anything compared to Charles the Great!

SMITH: No, but it's harder to shoe a horse so he doesn't wear out his shoes unevenly . . .

SCHOOLMASTER: Hafiz says very correctly in the third chapter, page seventy-eight, as follows: "Eat, man! You don't know when you'll get the chance again!"

SMITH: I simply want to say it's called *pagina* in Latin, just as one says Carolina, etc. Isn't it *pagina*?

SCHOOLMASTER: Yes, yes. Yes!

SMITH: Right is right—that's my principle. Do you know, Schoolmaster, when Julius Caesar was born? That'll get him!

SCHOOLMASTER: 99 B.C.

SMITH: Before the birth of Christ? That's impossible, because counting the years starts with year one, doesn't it, and one can't count backwards, can one?

SCHOOLMASTER: Why not?

SMITH: Watch it, don't start arguing! Watch it! You have such a poor head something could happen to it!—Can you tell me, Schoolmaster, what the difference between rye and wheat is?

SCHOOLMASTER: Julius Caesar was born in 99 and died in 31 . . .

SMITH: Listen to that! How could that be? Did he live backwards maybe?—The difference between rye and wheat is, first, the price of grain or market price, second, the tariffs protect rye but not wheat. Didn't I put that nicely?

SCHOOLMASTER: Yes, yes, yes!

SMITH: But the monetary standard, that's something else! I'm in favor of silver, I don't want to deny that, and the stock exchange, that's still something else, and market quotations is something else, too, and the exchange business is still something else . . .

SCHOOLMASTER: But what is it?

SMITH: What it is? Do I need to stand here telling you that? Don't I have other things to do? Haven't I paid my taxes? Am I not married? I just ask you! I just ask! If there's anyone who has something to criticize, I'll ask to talk privately with him, privately! Do you know what that is? Behind the barn. Don't say a word, I can't stand being answered, no one may ever answer me. Do you consider all these questions settled now, in my favor, or shall we go back of the barn? I'm a very serious man, but I'm not to be trifled with!—Now, gentlemen, you know what a jackass you have before you; I don't mean myself but the schoolmaster, who thinks someone can be born before the year one! But you're going to know thoroughly what sort of man he is!

Well, he's the stupidest creature that walks in two shoes; he's so stupid he thinks there are Guano Islands—surely there aren't any like that!—(*Takes up a bottle and takes a swig*) He doesn't know the difference between rye and wheat—and he drinks, too—you probably think I drink, too, but I only pop corks and that can't be called drinking, for that is something else.—Knowledge, gentlemen, that is a virtue, but the schoolmaster doesn't know anything, absolutely nothing, and they've put him in charge of educating children; but he's even a despot, a tyrant, a power-crazy wretch and a rowdy! Now you know who he is!

WANDERER: Hold it! I certainly don't intend to answer you; for then you'd get violent; I don't intend to question you, for then your knowledge would prove faulty; I don't intend to offer you a drink, for that's unnecessary, just as little as I'd want to argue with you, for you'd never understand what I meant, and you'd never admit I was right, but I'd like to ask you one thing.

SMITH: Ask, but ask nicely!

WANDERER: You're surely a character?

SMITH: I'm a real character, firm of character in a word.

WANDERER: And you're a silver man, too?

SMITH: I'm proud of being called a silver man.

WANDERER: You don't recognize gold as the standard in world trade?

SMITH: No! No gold!

WANDERER: And not in private use either?

SMITH: I have to think that over! (*Aside*) Does he intend to cheat me on the exchange? (*Aloud*) I won't answer that. I don't want to answer, no one can make me answer—and though I have a good mind, I still don't understand what you mean!

WANDERER: Still? ! Were you afraid your firmness of character wouldn't stand the test?

SMITH: Are you sitting slandering me? Don't, for I have absolute power here in the village; I'm a despot!

(*The* WANDERER *laughs.*)

SMITH: Don't look at me, for I'm a terrible despot!

WANDERER: I didn't look at you, I just laughed!

SMITH: Don't laugh! My tax base is six thousand and that's nothing to laugh at! I have five children, all well brought up, richly endowed, especially intellectually, two are in America, of course, ta! Things like that happen, and one has been guilty of a slip . . . but he has made up for that, so that's nothing to talk about, nothing at all!

WANDERER (*aside*): He is superb!

HUNTER: But this must end! I'm suffocating!

SMITH: I'm only going after my manuscript; then the festival can begin! But you may not go, gentlemen; I'm the mayor and have absolute command; the schoolmaster's going to read parts of his tragedy, *Potamogeton*, for the time being; it isn't so stupid considering it's by a dilettante, but many dogs are the rabbit's death!

SCHOOLMASTER: And the verses go of themselves just like big goslings.

SMITH: Was that a dig at me?

SCHOOLMASTER: It surely can't be since you're grownup!

SMITH: Full-fledged is the word for talking about birds; read nicely for these gentlemen now, and I'll be back right away; but don't slander me in my absence.

WANDERER: But that isn't possible in your presence, is it?

SMITH: That's true, and one chooses the least of two evils; so: slander me in my absence, but not in my presence! (*Goes*)

*

WANDERER: What sort of town is this? Is it an asylum?

SCHOOLMASTER: Yes, they're all so wicked they've gone crazy.

WANDERER: Is anyone keeping an eye on you here?

SCHOOLMASTER: I've been put under observation because they suspect I'm sane.

WANDERER: Come with us then and we'll escape!

SCHOOLMASTER: Then they'll take all three of us in!

WANDERER: So it isn't only a stupid joke?

SCHOOLMASTER: Wickedness is the mother of folly, and its child at the same time.

WANDERER: Who is this smith?

SCHOOLMASTER: He's a lord of flies, the kind Elijah[16] talks about; he is made up of the others' malice, envy, hate, and lies. The smith became mayor because the baker was the most deserving; when I had served faithfully for twenty-five years they celebrated the day by giving a party for the smith; at the latest festival of jackasses the smith got the laurel wreath, because he had written the poorest verse.

HUNTER: Better flee than fence badly; you can't fence here, so we'll flee!

WANDERER: We're really in danger for our lives here!

SCHOOLMASTER: But the most dangerous of all is to flee.

WANDERER: Can't we fool them since they're stupid?

SCHOOLMASTER: But they're cunning as all stupid people are—

WANDERER: We'll try!—Smith!

(*The* SMITH *enters.*)

WANDERER: Abra-cadabra, abra-cadabra!

SMITH: What can I do for you? Do you intend to leave? Don't! Really, don't do that!

WANDERER: We're only going to the next town to get requisites for the festival.

SMITH: What are you going to get?

WANDERER: Requisites.

SMITH: That's requisitions, I suppose; requisitions are always welcome. Are they goods for the smithy, especially?

WANDERER: They're shoenails and wheelhubs, scythes and spades . . .

SMITH: Splendid!

WANDERER: But we have to have the schoolmaster along to help us carry . . .

SMITH: He's very feeble, and he's simple-minded, too!

WANDERER: But requisitions are only pieces of paper, of course, and he's surely strong enough for them!

SMITH: Very true, very true . . . but wheelhubs are heavy; he won't manage those . . .

WANDERER: But requisitions for wheelhubs aren't heavier than requisitions for nails.

SMITH: Very true, very true . . . Well, go along! But be sure to come back!

WANDERER: Don't you understand that if one goes, one has to come back . . .

SMITH: Wait a minute: what is it that goes and goes and never comes back?

WANDERER: That's the watch, but we aren't watches, so we'll come back!

SMITH: That's logical, and I understand that! But wait a minute: your clocks won't come back then?

WANDERER: They aren't clocks but watches.

SMITH: Very true. Watches are something else. But wait a minute!

WANDERER: But we go, and that's the main thing!

SMITH: Quite right—that's the main thing! And it's logical; I like logic in all the circumstances of life; and I can follow only a strictly logical argument . . .

WANDERER: That's why you shouldn't come along, for we're not a logical argument.

SMITH: Quite right! So I'll stay at my post, and you'll go! Go on!

WANDERER: Sing the praises of the jackass, great rhyme-smith!
Wisest of all the animals on earth,
you have the finest hearing of all,
with your ears long as trumpets,
you hear how the grass grows under the stone,
and see into east and west at the same time;
your strength of character shows in your stiff legs,
your will is your master's law;
when you should stand, you gladly run,
and when you're whipped to run, you stand still.

SMITH: That's really very well said—for the mammal in question has belonged to the world of the misunderstood, the camp of the silent, and really deserved to be re-ha-bi-

WANDERER: -litated! But have you ever heard a silent jackass?

SMITH: No, but I don't pay any attention to that; I pay attention to its character, its strength of character, and that's why I understand the misunderstood mammal; I identify myself with it; yes, I do.

WANDERER: Do you stand by that?

SMITH: Yes, I stand by that!

WANDERER: Then we'll go!

SMITH: Wait a minute! I stand, but I don't stand alone, I have opinion and party; all right-thinking, enlightened, unprejudiced people—in a word: the nation gathers about my banner; and when I keep on standing here, I want to show you that you're wrong, because right is right. Isn't that logical?

SCHOOLMASTER: The highest right is the highest wrong!

SMITH: And the voice of the people is the voice of God!—Come in, people! Assemble, nation!

*

(PEOPLE *enter, just a few persons.*)

WANDERER: It's the nation, but they're so few!

SMITH: They *are* few, but you don't see the masses who stand back of them.

WANDERER: No, I can't see any!

SMITH: You don't see for the natural reason they are invisible! That's logical!—People! These learned charlatans insist there are some Guano Islands. Surely there isn't anything of the kind?

PEOPLE: No!

SMITH: So these gentlemen are liars or stupid asses!—Is there a punishment severe enough for such rascals who spread lies?

WANDERER: There is one that is more cruel than every other: that's exile!

SMITH: Well, that's not bad! But we must have complete evidence against them first.—One of them insists Homer nodded!

WANDERER: At times!

SMITH: At times or always, that's the same thing. That's sophistry. People, do you think a poet can sleep? Have you ever heard anything so idiotic?

ONE OF PEOPLE: But he surely slept at night!

SMITH: At night? Is that any answer? Have I permitted anyone to answer? Come back of the barn and I'll answer!

ONE OF PEOPLE: Is it a question of taking sides?

SMITH: Yes, a human being should take sides; otherwise, he's a characterless person who only vacillates.

*

SCHOOLMASTER: Won't you read from your Charles the Great,[17] Smith, so we get away from this squabble—these gentlemen are in a hurry, you see. (*Aside to the* HUNTER *and the* WANDERER) He isn't really Charles the Great, but we have to say that, otherwise we'll be locked up.

SMITH: I heard what he said! And I saw you gentlemen grinning, and the one who grins, agrees.—Put them in! You know what I mean.—Seize them!—His name wasn't Charles the Great, but we call him that because he was, quite simply, great!—Slap their mouths and lock them up until they come to a better way of thinking!

(*The* HUNTER, WANDERER, *and* SCHOOLMASTER *are seized and being taken away.*)

HUNTER: But we're exiled and should go to the next town for requisites . . .

SMITH: That's absolutely correct, everything's correct. You may go on your word of honor you'll come back and with the promise or rather on the promise you'll be grateful, for an ungrateful person is the heaviest burden Earth has. I have, you see, a wife who keeps open house, well, that probably sounds silly, but it's a literary salon, and I'll expect you gentlemen there at the first summons!

WANDERER: So we're free! But at what a price!

HUNTER: Is it freedom to be imprisoned by the chain of one's word of honor in a literary salon?

SMITH: Be off! But—the nation stays!

(*The* HUNTER, WANDERER, *and* SCHOOLMASTER *go.*)

[CURTAIN]

4

AN ARCADE IN THE CITY

The arcade in Thofeth.[18] *The first wing to the right a restaurant; the second a photographer's shop; the third a seashell shop; the first to the left flowers and fruit; the second a Japanese tea and perfume store.*

The HUNTER *and the* WANDERER *are sitting outside the florist shop.*

WANDERER: You're really depressed.

HUNTER: I've come too far down!

WANDERER: You've been in Thofeth before?

HUNTER: Yes, I've lived here.

WANDERER: I could tell.

HUNTER: We have to get some chloroform—my wounds are starting to ache!

WANDERER: *Vinum et circenses!* [19] Here we'll get a show free of charge; this seems to be the city's sewer through which everything pours! (*Signals to someone in the restaurant; a waitress comes and puts wine on their table.*) They'll recognize you here, I suppose?

HUNTER: That's impossible, for I've let my beard grow, cut my hair and washed my hands this morning. You see, in this town they can't recognize a person if he washes up!

WANDERER: But the waitress is looking at you.

HUNTER: I probably look like one of her old friends.

WANDERER: Here comes a little distraction—

(*The* ORGANGRINDER *enters with a monkey.*)

WANDERER: Come here, Musician, and we'll ransom our heads with an even sum.

ORGANGRINDER: Heads?

WANDERER: Well, our ears, then! Here's a gold coin for you if you don't play!

ORGANGRINDER: But it's the monkey that's the main attraction!

WANDERER: Then we'll look at her but without accompaniment.

ORGANGRINDER: But there's music for . . .

WANDERER: Is it true that you people in this town are descendants of a monkey?[20]

ORGANGRINDER: *If* it's true? Watch it!

WANDERER: When I take a closer look at you, I, too, believe it's true!—I'm sure of it; I'll swear to it! May I see the music?—Well, but this Zeus head looks more like a ram.

ORGANGRINDER: Yes-s, it really does! Well, then it's probably so!

WANDERER: Do you really think that mammal in the red coat who's shooting with a pistol is the father of the human race?

ORGANGRINDER: If you're a freethinker, you'd better watch it. . . . We're orthodox here in this city and are the defenders of the faith.

WANDERER: Which faith?

ORGANGRINDER: The only true faith: the theory of evolution.

*

HUNTER: Now we'll probably be charged with blasphemy!—Where did the schoolmaster go?

WANDERER: He disappeared as soon as he had used us, of course.

HUNTER: Shall we leave?

WANDERER: How would that help? It can't make much difference if we fall into the hands of these people or some others!

HUNTER: For human beings lie along highways like robbers spying on each other. Look through the restaurant window, where the waitress is standing staring at you with beseeching eyes as if she were begging you to take her into your care out of mercy! She's pretty and can stir up feelings other than pity! Just assume you'd think it over and free her from her heavy, rather humiliating work in there; assume you'd offer her a home, protect her from the worst blows in life; she'd in short order rob you of friends, take you away from your family, insult your superiors and patrons—in a word, eat you up,

WANDERER: and if I didn't permit that, she'd sue me for assault and battery,

HUNTER: and for ruining her youth . . . but the worst would be you'd get into a family you don't know,

WANDERER: but which I sense. . . . Imagine, she's standing in there pulling and drawing at me . . . stirring up a whirlwind; she's spinning a net which feels like warm air. . . . Wait a minute, I'll go in and tear it to pieces,

HUNTER: or be caught in it.

(*The* WANDERER *goes into the restaurant.*)

∗

HUNTER (*alone*): A man overboard!—

∗

PHOTOGRAPHER (*comes up to him with a camera*): May I take your picture, sir?

HUNTER: No!

PHOTOGRAPHER: Do me that favor—I'm very poor.

HUNTER: But you may not display me in the showcase, on a cigarette package, or on soap wrappers;[21] and if I get to look like an Australian aborigine or the latest mass murderer, you're to destroy the plate!

PHOTOGRAPHER: You're very suspicious, sir . . .

HUNTER: Not at all, but I'm a little careful!

(*The* PHOTOGRAPHER *signals toward the shop. His* WIFE [EUPHROSYNE] *comes out.*)

*

PHOTOGRAPHER: May I present my wife? She generally helps with developing and printing. Come on, Euphrosyne; I've promised to take a picture of this gentleman in spite of being too busy—come on, Euphrosyne, talk to the gentleman while I'm working!

EUPHROSYNE (*sits down*): You're lucky, sir, to have found an artist like my husband . . . he's the ablest *I* have seen, and if that picture doesn't turn out well, you may say *I* don't understand art! So you should really appreciate his work and not act as if you're doing us a favor!

HUNTER: Just a minute . . .

EUPHROSYNE: Well, you shouldn't look so proud; when a person asks a favor of someone else, he ought to be grateful.

HUNTER: Wait a minute . . .

PHOTOGRAPHER (*calls out*): Gotthard!—Come here! You put the plates in backwards in the cassette . . .

GOTTHARD (*comes out*): I didn't put any plates in the cassette . . .

EUPHROSYNE: Are you going to talk back to your father, your own father?

GOTTHARD: I don't even know what a cassette is. . . . I deal in seashells . . .

PHOTOGRAPHER: You deal, yes; but do you sell any? Ask this
gentleman if he needs any seashells; I thought he said
something about seashells a while ago. . . .

HUNTER: I haven't said a word about seashells; I spoke of
cigarette packages and soap wrappers . . .

EUPHROSYNE: Gotthard, bring the cigarettes. Didn't you hear
the gentleman wants some?

HUNTER: I wanted to get out of having my picture on a
cigarette package and on a soap wrapper. . . .

GOTTHARD (*sits down*): I can understand you're hard to deal
with, but let's talk this over a little and we can arrange
it. . . .

EUPHROSYNE: You're right, Gotthard; we'll let him in on our
circumstances and he'll understand; ask Klara to come
out. . . .

GOTTHARD (*calls out*): Klara!

*

(KLARA, *the girl in the flower shop, comes out.*)

EUPHROSYNE: Try to sell a flower to this gentleman; he's so
thrifty or rather so stingy he doesn't even want to buy a
seashell even though Gotthard has the most beautiful *I*
have ever seen.

KLARA (*sits down*): Maybe you can talk to him even though he
looks stuck up. Is he a hunter?

EUPHROSYNE: You can surely see that.

KLARA: You kill animals. You mustn't do that, for it's a sin,
but you look cruel, too, like all drunkards; yes, the one
who drinks in the morning is a drunkard. . . .

HUNTER (*to* KLARA): What have you done with your
husband? (KLARA *frightened.*) It's a sin to kill
people!—Don't you know that?

KLARA: You mean?

HUNTER: Yes, that's what I mean!

KLARA: Witnesses, did you hear that he means?

ALL: Yes, we heard!

HUNTER: May I say one word? Merely one?

GOTTHARD: Nah! Why should we let you?

HUNTER: I don't intend to say what you're thinking, but something quite different.

EUPHROSYNE (*curious*): Say it then!

HUNTER: Has Möller been arrested yet?

(*All rise in horror.*)

*

WANDERER (*comes out of the café*): What's up?

HUNTER: Has Möller been arrested yet? (*All leave, threatening the* HUNTER.) The third time!—Has Möller been arrested?

(*All disappear.*)

*

WANDERER: What did that mean?

HUNTER: That was the town's secret! Everyone knows Möller committed the latest murder, but no one dares to testify because they lack evidence. We have to leave because of the bomb I've thrown.—Come!

WANDERER: I can't!

HUNTER: Caught?

WANDERER: In a tavern, drops in the glasses, matches and cigar ashes, pawed by young fellows, soaked with smoke, weary from late nights, and in spite of, in spite of everything, snared . . .

HUNTER: Tear yourself free!

WANDERER: I can't!

HUNTER: Then let's flee!

WANDERER: I can't!

HUNTER: Well, then stay!

WANDERER: I can't!—I can't do anything!

HUNTER: Then I'll say goodbye . . .

WANDERER: We'll meet again . . .

HUNTER: People always do, if they've only met once.
WANDERER: Goodbye then! (*Goes into the café.*)

                    *

HUNTER (*alone; walks about in the arcade, stops without purpose
     at the* PHOTOGRAPHER'*s shop*):
     This was really mine . . .
     a long time ago! My journey
     in the rain under this roof of glass;
     when soft yellow daylight made its impress,
     lighted candles always flamed in here,
     and flowers, fruits delighted my eye;
     and seashells whispered tales from the sea;
     in this shop pictures of acquaintances
     and half-acquaintances,
     were my company in loneliness!
     One look, one word was enough for me
     to feel kinship with mortal men. . . .
     They're still there. . . . Here's my oldest friend,
     he's surely gray, but his picture—
     as leaves in autumn—
     only has turned yellow—.
     Here I see relatives, former relatives—
     a brother-in-law who is no longer that—
     and here!—Oh, Savior of the world, help me!
     For I perish!—My child! [22]
     My child who is not mine,
     has been, but is not anymore!
     Someone else's! And yet mine!—
     And here is my café!
     Our table! So very long ago—
     all this has ceased to be,
     but still *is*—in my memory!
     The fire that can't be put out,

which burns, but doesn't warm—
which burns but does not burn up. . . .

*

(*The old* JAPANESE *comes out of the teashop; he looks as if he were dying. The* HUNTER *comes up to support him.*)

JAPANESE: A human being, at last! From where, to where?

HUNTER: From the great highway. Can I help you?

JAPANESE: Help me die.

HUNTER: One always has time for that.

JAPANESE: Don't say that; I can't live any longer; I have no one to turn to for the last favors, for in this Thofeth there isn't one human being . . .

HUNTER: What favors do you mean?

JAPANESE: You're to hold my sword, while I . . .

HUNTER: I don't want to do that! Why must you die?

JAPANESE: Because I can live no longer.

HUNTER: Tell me your long story in a few brief words.

JAPANESE: Yes!—Yes!—I left my country . . . because I had committed a wicked deed—I came here firmly intending to become an honorable human being by strict observation of the laws of honor and conscience—I sold quality goods at reasonable prices; but the inhabitants of this community liked only false goods at low prices. Then I had only one choice or go under. Instead of distilling the fragrances of flowers, I sold chemicals, and instead of the leaves of the teaplant, they got the leaves of blackthorn and cherry. At first my conscience didn't object—I had to live, of course!—But one day fifteen years ago I woke up; it seemed to me then as if everything I had lived and done was recorded in a book; and now the book was being opened. Day and night, night and day I read all the false entries, all the irregularities; and I have fought, but in vain. Death alone can set me free, for most of the evil is in my flesh: I have purified my soul through suffering——

HUNTER: In what way can I help you?

JAPANESE: In this!— I'll take a sleeping potion so that I seem dead—you will put me into a coffin, which will be brought to the crematory . . .

HUNTER: But if you wake up—?

JAPANESE: That's just what I'm counting on! For one moment I want to feel the purifying, redeeming power of fire—suffer a short while—and so experience the bliss of release—

HUNTER: And then?

JAPANESE: Then you're to gather my ashes in my most precious vase . . .

HUNTER: And put your name on it. . . . What is your name?

JAPANESE: Wait!—I have journeyed, erred, and suffered under the name Hiroshima, my birthplace. But in my country, when a person dies he discards his old cursed, dirtied name and gets a new one, which is called his eternity name. That alone is put on his gravestone along with a saying, after one has sacrificed a branch of the sakaki tree for the dead man.

HUNTER: Do you have this name ready?

JAPANESE: Yes, I do!—Here it is!

HUNTER: What does it mean?

JAPANESE: Harahara to. It means: "quivering leaves, rustling silk"—but it also means "falling tears."

HUNTER: And this saying?

JAPANESE: *Chiru hana wo—*
nanika uramin—
Yo no naka ni—
waga ni tomo ni—
aramu no kawa—

HUNTER: And that is interpreted?

JAPANESE: The flowers falling—

Why should I be angry?
Even I—along with them—
must by the gods' will perish!

HUNTER: I will fulfill your last wish. . . . But don't you have any survivors?

JAPANESE: I did once! I had a daughter who came here three years ago when she thought I was going to die. She came to inherit from me. But when I didn't die, she became furious—couldn't conceal her feelings—and left. With that she was dead for me.

HUNTER: Where shall what we talked about take place?

JAPANESE: Outside the city—at the crematory.

HUNTER: Shall we go out there together or meet there?

JAPANESE: We'll meet in the arbor at the inn . . . after a while. I shall only shave and bathe. . . .

HUNTER: Fine! Then we'll meet there!

JAPANESE (*nodding, goes toward the shop*): There comes the murderer!—Take care!

HUNTER: It is he?

JAPANESE: Take care! He's the most powerful man in town—. (*Goes*)

                              *

MURDERER (MÖLLER, *enters; stiff, arrogant, with his arms somewhat awkwardly at his sides; stares at the* HUNTER): Isn't it?

HUNTER: No, it isn't!

MURDERER: Well, then it's . . .

HUNTER: No; has been. . . . The one you mean no longer exists. . . .

MURDERER: So you're dead?

HUNTER: Yes!—Twelve years ago I committed hara-kiri;[23] I executed my old self, and the one you see here you do not know, can never get to know!

MURDERER: Yes, I remember you were stupid enough . . . to get up on the pillory to confess publicly, on the scarlet carpet, all your faults and weaknesses. . . .

HUNTER: And the whole community enjoyed it, all of them felt they were better people, and thought themselves made righteous through my public, civil death. They had neither a word of sympathy nor approval for my confession of sins.

MURDERER: Why should they have had?

HUNTER: After ten years of suffering when I had set things right, it occurred to me that I ought to confess your sins, too![24] Then there was another tune. . . .

MURDERER: You could've been damn sure of that!

HUNTER: You, for example, who committed a murder . . .

MURDERER: One doesn't say things like that when one doesn't have proof . . .

HUNTER: I know you're the most powerful man in the community, that you tyrannize even the grand duke, and all this on the basis of a gang of freemasons that exists here. . . .

MURDERER: What's that?

HUNTER: You know very well!—A league—which isn't the holy one . . .

MURDERER: What about you?

HUNTER: I have never belonged to the gang—but I recognize it by certain signs . . .

MURDERER: Take a look in the stationery shop window and you'll see who you are!

HUNTER: You mean that caricature? That's not I; that's you. That's what you look like inside. That's your creation! Help yourself!

MURDERER: You have a gift for shaking off vermin!

HUNTER: Do it, too, but not on me!—Execute yourself, as I did, had to do, when you made me the scapegoat on which you heaped all your sins!

MURDERER: What are you after?

HUNTER: For example: once upon a time there was a heretic, who wrote this bit of stupidity: that if he stood alone on Gaurisankar Mountain,[25] and the flood of sin came and drowned humanity, no harm would be done, just so *he* lived. At the next carnival Gaurisankar was carried in the procession, and on top of it *I* stood, not the heretic. What do you say to that?—And on my birthday, *he* was honored!—When I invented the new insulators, *you* got the prize! But when you committed murder, I was accused! Just the same, when the price of sugar went up on the exchange, they blamed my insulators, although you had got the prize as the inventor. If you can imagine anything so topsy turvy, twice over, then you have to stand on your head first and then turn around.

MURDERER: Do you have any proof since you dare call me murderer?

HUNTER: Yes, I do!

(MURDERER *amazed.*)

HUNTER: But I don't dare to use it before a jury of your friends, because they'd deny facts and have me arrested.—Tell me, who is the girl in there, the one who caught my companion?

MURDERER: She is—*your* daughter!

HUNTER: (*his hand over his heart, turns pale, and, his handkerchief, when he puts it to his mouth, gets red from blood.*): This child that you have brought up!—Now I'm going to the crematory! (*Goes out*)

[CURTAIN]

5

IN THE PARK OUTSIDE THE CREMATORY

Outside the Columbarium; an avenue of cypresses leads to the back. A bench, a chair, a table.
HUNTER (*enters alone*):
What do I see? A host of urns;
but all alike?
A pharmacy, a museum? No!
A columbarium, a dovecote;
but no dove, no olive branch—
only chaff, the grain grows somewhere else;
ashes in the urns, all alike
as speck of dust resembles speck of dust—
human lives now over—
and numbered, with labels—
"Here rests"—Yes, I knew you,
but you never got to know yourself. . .
and you, you went about disguised
through your long heavy life;
and when I stripped you, you died!
Worshipper of idols![26] That was your name,
your character! You forced one to adore
your horrid mate and your detestable sons;
one had to, or else one was sacrificed
and cut up with a knife every Saturday,
and lynched besides in the Sunday number—
robbed of bread and honor!
(*The* MURDERER *has entered and is listening.*)
HUNTER: You, the light of Thofeth, you collected the nation
about your bier; and although dead,

you could count the wreaths,
threatened him who had sent none!
MURDERER: That *is* nice by a grave!
HUNTER: It's no grave, it's a jar with a bit of dirt in it!—No, a stone! He gradually turned to stone . . .
MURDERER: You mean he died of hardening—
HUNTER: To limestone, yes!
MURDERER: Say a little about yourself!
HUNTER: I did just that thirteen years ago, so you're tired of that. But here are the ashes of a man I could say good things about, except that he was murdered and because he was murdered by you!

Your victim never did evil for the sake of evil, only in self-defense, and when he didn't want to be an accomplice in crime, he was killed, annihilated.
MURDERER: You associate with that scoundrel the Japanese . . .
HUNTER: Do you intend to strike me down now as "the great light" did?
MURDERER: Don't say anything bad about the dead; say "poor soul."
HUNTER: You always say that about scoundrels, whose fingers get caught in the sugar bowl . . . but never about your victims . . . be off with you now . . . quickly!
MURDERER: I'll go when I want to!

(*The* HUNTER *brings out his bloody handkerchief and shows it.*)
MURDERER (*turns away and is leaving*): I can't bear the sight of blood; that's a peculiarity of mine!
HUNTER: Since the fourth of April!

(*The* MURDERER *slowly leaves.*)
HUNTER (*to the* JAPANESE): Are you ready for the journey?
JAPANESE: I am; but let us sit down
until the oven has been heated!

HUNTER: With pleasure!
(*They sit down.*)
Tell me, now that life lies at your feet
as a wounded deer, hunted, caught,
how does your journey seem?
JAPANESE: (*after a pause*):
A stroke with many twists
as the copy of the writing
the blotter records—reversed—
now ahead, now back, up and down
but seen in the mirror it can be read—
HUNTER: What was the hardest to bear?
of all the stones that bruised your foot?
JAPANESE (*thinks*):
I spared an enemy once—
and later he struck me down!—
You see, to have to regret any good
one has done—that is among the worst!

Another time I uttered kind words
to one depressed!—He became my enemy—
he took everything away from me
and I was helpless in an uneven struggle:
for he had in writing my word
that he was a better human being than I!

But all that is as nothing though,
nothing compared to the fact of life itself—
the humility of wandering
a bare skeleton clothed in flesh,
and set going with sinews, cords,
by a tiny motor in the chest's
engine room, propelled by the heat
the stomach's furnace can get up—

and the soul, the spirit sits in the heart
like a bird in the cage of one's breast,
a basket or a net.

Little bird, I'll soon open the cage,
and you may fly—to your home,
to the isles of flowers and sun,
where you were born,
but did not get to die!
See! My best vase, a family heirloom,
which shall house the dust from dust—
but with flowers in it
it decked the table set
for feasting, where young eyes
and glowing cheeks were mirrored
in glass with golden edges—
and a little hand served the children
the good things of the house—

Then you became a flask for tears, dear vase!
For everything that life gave us of good
became the source of tears.

I remember, it was at New Year's
when the children had their festival of dolls—
in our land we keep all dolls from generation to
generation—

A child!
What could be more perfect of its kind
than this little creature?
Not man, not woman,
but both, and neither—
a human being in miniature.

Tell me, Wanderer; I have forgotten you
because of my sorrows—say one word
about yourself! About your lot—
How does life look to you, and how did it look?
What did you find hardest, most bitter?
HUNTER: This I found more bitter than death—
to have to take the great comedy seriously—
to consider that sacred which was coarse!

When I smiled at the comedy, I had to weep;
and when in the coarseness I became coarse,
I had to be ashamed!

And this!
I was a preacher, of course;
I began by speaking well of people,
pulled out all the beauty I knew,
and set high goals in life—
They're called ideals—
bright banners set as signals—
which gather people for holiday and feast.—
But now—how very bitter—all the beauty I've thought
and spoken—I have to take back!
Beauty does not exist in life—
cannot be realized down here—
and the ideal does not actually exist.
JAPANESE: I know it—but it is a memory,
a hope, a beacon to sail by—
and therefore: full sails ahead!
Let the banners stream out,
they're way up, but can be better seen . . .
and show the way up—toward the sun!
HUNTER: The oven is beginning to glow . . .
JAPANESE: And throws a rosy glow on the tops

of the cypress as the light of morning
when the sun comes up—
Welcome, day! Farewell, night!
With your heavy dreams!
For the last time I undress
and go to rest, fall asleep—

And when I wake—I am with my mother,
my wife, my child, my friends!
Good night, poor human being! (*Goes*)
(*The stage is now illuminated and one sees in the clouds the
same image—as in the first scene—of the Land of Desires.*)

[CURTAIN]

6

AT THE LAST GATE

*At the back two white gates opening toward a low sandy
beach and the blue sea.*

*To the left a red country house (a hunting lodge) in a beech
wood; to the left a hornbeam hedge and an orchard.*

Outside the house a small table has been set for a namesday[27]
celebration.

*Above the hornbeam hedge a ball can be seen being thrown up
and down.*

*A baby carriage with a blue hood thrown back is next to the
gate.*

HUNTER (*enters, deep in thought*):
Yes!—Alone!—That is the end,
when one wants to keep his life
and not to use it in exchange
to buy his way to a position—
not to let oneself be stolen,
not to let oneself be controlled . . .
When first my thoughts awakened,
and it became clear to me
that I was locked up in a madhouse,
a prison, a house of correction,
I wished I'd lose my mind
so no one would sense what I was thinking—
"*Teló, teló manänai!*"[28]
I want, I want to be mad!
And wine became my friend—
in the mists of drink I hid my self,
in the fool's garb of drink, people forgot me,
and did not suspect who I was—.
Now it has changed,
the drink of forgetfulness has become memory's—
I remember everything, everything—
the seals are broken, the books opened!
Of themselves they read aloud;
and when my ear wearies, I see;
I see everything, everything!
    (*Comes to*)
Where have I come? The sea?
And a beech wood, a hunter's cottage—
and there a ball that rises, falls;
a little carriage, with a newborn child,
the hood like the blue vault of the sky
placed over the sleep of innocence;
in the red house back of green shutters,

a happy pair have hid themselves
have concealed their happiness!
For there is happiness, no doubt of that,
but brief, as the flash of lightning,
as sunshine, as the morning glory—
one blossom and *one* day,
and then the end!—
There rises the chimney smoke from the kitchen,
with a well-stocked storehouse in back,
a little cellar underneath,
a bright veranda toward the woods—
I know how it should be—
how it has been! . . .
And here a namesday table set
for the little girl!
A little altar to childhood,
to hope, to innocent joy,
based on one's own happiness,
and not on others' misfortunes—
and there's the beach
with white, pure, soft, warm sand—
with seashells, pebbles,
and the blue water to splash in
with bare feet . . .
Leaves have been spread, the walks raked,
company's expected—a children's party!
They've watered the flowers—
the flowers of my childhood.
The blue monkshood with two doves in it—
the crown-imperial with its diadem,
and the scepter and the apple—.
The flower of passion, of suffering
in white and amethyst, with the cross,
and the lance, and the nails—

visited by eager bees, that out of its chalice
can fetch honey
where we find only bile—
and there the loveliest of all trees
in the children's paradise!
Among the dark green leaves peer forth
the beautiful berries, two and two—
with the cherry's red and white cheeks—
tiny children's faces—brother and sister!
who play, caress each other when the wind sways them
. . .
And between the branch and stem, an orchard warbler
has built its home—
invisible singer, a song on wings . . .
Sh-h! The sand crunches under a small shoe,
here comes the little girl!

                                       *

CHILD (*enters; takes the* HUNTER *by the hand and leads him up to the baby carriage*): Walk quietly, so you may look at the doll!—There's the doll! For that's what we call her!—But you mustn't walk in the sand, for it has been raked!—Ellen has raked, for we're going to have company!—It's my namesday today—
    Are you sad?
HUNTER: What's your name, Child?
CHILD: My name's Maria.
HUNTER: Who lives in that house?
CHILD: Papa and mama.
HUNTER: May I see your namesday table?
CHILD: But we mayn't touch anything . . .
HUNTER: No, I won't touch anything! Dear child.
CHILD: Do you know what we're going to have for dinner today?—Asparagus and strawberries! Why are you sad?

Have you lost your money? You may take a favor on the table, but you mayn't take the big one, for Stella's to have that. Did you know Stella got bread crumbs in her bed last night, and then she cried, and then it thundered so we got afraid and mama closed the damper! Well, she was eating a sandwich in bed, and the sandwich went to pieces, for it was crumbly store bread—that they buy in town—

Now we're going to tell a story. Can you tell a story? What's your name?

HUNTER: My name's . . . Cartaphilus.[29]

CHILD: No, you don't have a name like that . . .

HUNTER: Ahasuerus[30] then! Who wanders and wanders . . .

CHILD: Now we'll talk about something else—Do your eyes hurt?

HUNTER: Yes, dear, very, very much—

CHILD: You shouldn't read in bed! Then your eyes hurt.

(A bugle is heard.)

CHILD: Papa's coming! (*Goes out*)

*

HUNTER: My child!

My child!

She didn't know me! How lucky . . . how lucky for us both!

Farewell, lovely vision,
I'll not stand in the way of the sun,
and throw shadows on the little ones' garden—
I know the father here—and the mother, too—
lovely simile, a simile
that limps, but is lovely!
A memory perhaps, or more than that:
a hope—a summer day in the forest
by the sea—a namesday table and a cradle!

A ray of sunlight from a child's eyes,
a gift from a tiny hand—
And so forward again and out—into the darkness!

[CURTAIN]

7

THE DARK FOREST

A dark forest.

HUNTER: Alone!—I've lost my way—In the darkness!
"And Elijah sat down under a juniper tree and wishes that
he might die: 'It is enough! Take away my life, O Lord!'"[31]
VOICE (*in the darkness*): He who would lose his life, shall keep
it.
HUNTER: Who is it that speaks out of the darkness?
VOICE: Is it dark?
HUNTER: Is it dark?
WOMAN (*enters*): I ask because I cannot see—I am blind!
HUNTER: Have you always been blind?
WOMAN: No! When I could weep no longer, my eyes
stopped seeing!
HUNTER: It is good to be able to weep!
WOMAN: But I hear instead, and I know your voice! . . .
I know who you are!
I believe in you!
HUNTER: You should not believe in me, not in any human
being; you should believe in God.

WOMAN: I believe in Him, too!

HUNTER: But believe only in God. The children of men are nothing to believe in . . .

WOMAN: Were you a lawyer?

HUNTER: I was the advocate for the Only True One against the worshippers of idols—You always wanted to worship yourselves, your relatives, your friends—but you never wanted to grant simple justice—

WOMAN: There were times when you deserted the cause you were defending!

HUNTER: When people fooled me into sympathizing with an unrighteous person with the excuse that he was a pitiable human being, I deserted the unrighteous person's cause—

WOMAN: You believed in the gospel once but tired of it!

HUNTER: I didn't tire; but when I discovered that I couldn't practice what I preached, I quit preaching so that I wouldn't be called a hypocrite!—And when I discovered there wasn't any application in practice of the beautiful ideals, I put their attainment in the land of fulfilled desires!

WOMAN: And now you're dead?

HUNTER: Yes, socially dead, but not spiritually! I'm struggling, therefore I'm alive! *I* do not exist; only what I have done, that exists! Good and bad! I have confessed what is bad and have suffered for it, have tried to make up for it by doing good!

WOMAN: Do you still want to plead the cause of human beings?

HUNTER: When they're right, otherwise not!———I defended a man's case once, misled by the gratitude I owed him; but by doing that I happened to do an innocent man a great injustice.—That's how it is with our best feelings, too—they fool us into committing wicked deeds!

WOMAN: *You* accuse . . . the accuser!

HUNTER: Whom do I accuse?

WOMAN: The one in control!

HUNTER: Get thee behind me, Satan! Before you tempt me into blasphemy!

WOMAN: Satan?

HUNTER: Yes, Satan!

WOMAN: No one was as black as you.

HUNTER: Because you denigrated me to make me like the rest of you.—But explain this: when *I* confessed *my* sins, you felt yourselves free of sins and thanked God you were not like me, even though you were at least as shabby as I.

As a child I saw an execution—the mob was like a mass of hypocrites; and when they went home, they pitied themselves; and on their way home, they went into taverns and said nasty things about the dead man, and thereby implied they were better than he was. . . . But afterwards some went back to Gallows Hill and took some of the dead man's blood—to cure epilepsy; they dipped their handkerchiefs into his blood—look at this one! (*Holds up his own bloody handkerchief.*) It's true you're blind!—Touch it—your eye is in your hand.

WOMAN (*touching it*): It feels red—but it's sticky—and it smells like—a butcher shop.—No, now I have it.—A relative died recently who coughed up—first, his lungs, finally his heart itself.

HUNTER: He *coughed* up his heart?

WOMAN: Yes!

HUNTER (*looks at the handkerchief*): I believe!

As you know, the buck isn't a clean animal, but on the day of the great redemption he got all the sins of humanity cast upon him; and loaded down in that way he was driven into the wilderness to be devoured by wild animals! That was the scapegoat!

WOMAN: Do you think you have suffered for other people's sins?

HUNTER: For my own *and* others'; therefore, even others'.

WOMAN: Weren't you something else before you became an advocate?

HUNTER: Yes, I was an architect! I built many houses, all weren't good ones, but when I built well, people became angry with me because I built well! So they gave the work to others, who did poorer work! That was in the city of Thofeth, where I built the theater.[32]

WOMAN: It's considered beautiful!

HUNTER: Remember that then when I'm dead—and forget me!

WOMAN: "I *do* not *exist*, only the good I have done *exists*."

Why did you never have any sympathy for your fellow human beings?

HUNTER: The question isn't properly put! Did you ever see anyone who had sympathy for me? No!—How could I respond to feelings, which were not extended to me?—And besides, who was the first one to preach: "Human beings are to be pitied!"

(*The* WOMAN *disappears*.)

*

HUNTER: She left!

They always leave when one wants to defend oneself!

*

TEMPTER (*enters*): There you are! Let's have a talk, but it's a little dark so we'll light up—(*It becomes lighter*.)—so we can see each other—it's very necessary we can see each other when we're going to talk sense.

The message is from the grand duke, he appreciates you because of your talents—he's offering you a position as court architect with such and such a salary, a residence with heating and upkeep, etc., you understand!

HUNTER: I don't want any position—

TEMPTER: Wait a minute, but on the condition, that, well—in

a word, you behave like a human being, an ordinary human being.

HUNTER: Would you tell me? I'd be interested in knowing how an ordinary human being behaves!

TEMPTER: Don't you know that?—Why do you look so crazy?

HUNTER: I'll answer the last question in few words: I look crazy because I've been driven crazy. You see, I belong to the kind of people, who believe what others say, right off; therefore I've been filled with lies. Everything I've believed in was a lie; that's why my whole being has become false; I have wandered about with false notions about people and about life, calculated with wrong terms, handed out false coins without knowing it; that's why I'm not the one I am.

I cannot be among other people, not talk, not quote another person's words, not appeal to a statement, for fear that it's a lie! Several times I've become an accomplice in that smithy which is called the community, but when I got like the others, I went out to become a highwayman, an outlaw.

TEMPTER: That's just talk—now we'll go back to the grand duke, who asks for your services.

HUNTER: He doesn't ask for my services, but for my soul . . .

TEMPTER: He asks that you devote your interests to his great undertakings . . .

HUNTER: I can't. . . . Leave now—I don't have much time left to live and want to be alone to settle my accounts . . .

TEMPTER (*laughs*):
If the day of payment has come,
then I'll come with invoices—
with bills and summons—

HUNTER:
Yes, come! Come with despair,

Lars Hanson and Olof Widgren in *The Great Highway* (Royal Dramatic Theater, Stockholm, 1949)

Harriet Bosse
i „Kronbruden"

P.H.
1738

Fanny Falkner in *Swanwhite* (The Intimate Theater, Stockholm, 1908)

Opposite, Harriet Bosse in *The Crownbride* (Royal Dramatic Theater, Stockholm, 1901)

August Strindberg

Tempter, who wants to fool me
into cowardly denial of the good giver!

I descended from the pure air of the mountains
to wander yet a while among the children of men—
and share in their little troubles;
but there was no open road, only
a ravine between thorny thickets—
I was caught fast in the bushes—
and left a shred here and a shred there;
they offered in order to take back with interest,
they gave to make the gift a debt—
they helped to gain control
they freed to gain the right to bind—
I lost my companion on the way—
the one snare followed upon the other—
and I was drawn into the millwheel—
came out on the other side—
Caught a gleam from a child's eye
that led me—to this place in the darkness.
Now you come with the bills—
What's that? Even he has disappeared!

So I am alone!
In night and darkness!
The trees sleep and the grass weeps
with cold since the sun set,
but the animals keep watch, but not all,
the nighthawk spins its plots,
and the snake twists under the poisonous mushroom—
and the badger, shy of light, moves
having slept through the day—
Alone!—Why?—
A traveler in a foreign land

is always a foreigner, alone.
He goes through cities, villages,
puts up, pays, and goes on—
till the journey's over—then he's home!

But it isn't over . . .
I still hear . . . a withered branch
that cracks—and an iron heel against a stone—
that is the terrifying smith,
idol worshipper with his knife—
he's seeking me—
and the miller with his wheel
where I was drawn in—
and almost was caught—
the people in the arcade, those people,
a net, easy to be caught in
but hard to get out of.—
And the murderer Möller—
with his bills and summons—
and alibi, and libel—
that infamous soul!
What do I now hear?—Music!
I know your strains, and your little hand!
I don't long to meet you—
for the fire warms at a pleasant distance,
but not too close, for then it scorches!
And now: a child's voice in the darkness!
Dear child, my last bright memory,
which follows me into the night forest!
On the last journey to that distant land—
the land of wishes fulfilled,
a mirage from the Alpine height,
but hidden in the valleys—
by highway dust, by chimney smoke!

Where did you go, beautiful vision,
land of longing, land of dreams?

If only a vision, I want to see you
from a snowy height, in crystal clear air—
at the hermit's; there I'll stay
and await release!
He'll surely give me a pit
under the cold white blanket:
and then write in the snow a fleeting epitaph:
Here rests Ishmael, son of Hagar,[33]
who once was called Israel,
because he had had to fight with God,
and did not give up until brought low,
overcome by the goodness of His might!
O eternal God! I will not let go Your hand,[34]
Your hard hand, before You bless me!
Bless me, bless your humanity,
which suffers, suffers from the gift of Life!
Me first, who has suffered most—
who has suffered most from the agony
of being unable to be what I wanted to be!

[CURTAIN]

Notes on
'The Great Highway'

1. The title of the play refers—on the symbolic level—to the journey along the pathways through life with their "road signs," flaws, and the like. Norrtullsgatan was the main road from Stockholm north to Uppsala, and the road was known in Strindberg's day as *Stora landsvägen*, literally "the great highway." The Strindbergs lived—during his boyhood—in various houses on or near that street.

2. *Chrysaëtos* is also the name of one of Strindberg's best known poems, a poem in which he deals with his love for a woman. The Greek word *chryso's* means "gold."

3. *Quo vadis*, the Latin for "whither (where) are you going?"

4. *Excelsior*, the Latin motto meaning "higher," "upwards," or "toward the heights."

5. In Miguel de Cervantes Saavedra's novel *Don Quixote* (1605), the author attacked, among other matters, one-sided idealism which disregards reality and also the limitations of selfish common sense.

6. Aphrodite or Venus, goddess of love and beauty, according to Greek mythology, was born fullgrown in the foam of the sea, the daughter of Zeus and Dione.

7. Strindberg was well acquainted with literary accounts of the philosophy of clothes, not least Swedenborg's. Here the reference is to Genesis 3:7: "And the eyes of them both were opened, and they knew that they were naked; and they sewed fig leaves together, and made themselves aprons."

8. See Genesis 27 for the account of Esau's loss of his birthright.

74

9. See, for example, St. Luke 23, for an account of the Jewish King Herod, the Roman governor Pontius Pilate, and the trial of Christ.

10. The North Star.

11. Flower games.

12. Translated in the immediately following words.

13. *Potamogeton* are pondweeds. The satiric implication is obvious: An impressive sounding title, but lowly, even worthless matter.

14. Verner von Heidenstam's *Karolinerna* (1898), translated as *The Charles Men.* Strindberg considered Charles XII responsible for bringing Sweden's time as a great power to an end.

15. The Chincha Islands off the coast of Peru.

16. Beelzebub. See I Kings and II Kings.

17. *The Charles Men.* See n. 14.

18. Stockholm is Thofeth, a place where human beings are sacrificed.

19. Wine and games (entertainment of a distracting kind).

20. The theory of evolution, which suggests man evolved from the apes.

21. The exploitation of a person's achievements or fame through advertising.

22. Strindberg's youngest child, Anne-Marie (born 1902), the daughter of Harriet Bosse, his third wife.

23. In his confessional dramas, *To Damascus, I, II,* and *III,* and in his autobiographical novels from *Inferno* on, Strindberg had testified publicly about his own faults and weaknesses.

24. Many of his post-Inferno works are testimony about his fellow human beings' faults and weaknesses, sins of omission and commission.

25. A mountain peak in the Himalayas.

26. Gustaf af Geijerstam, the object of Strindberg's bitter attack in *The Gothic Rooms* and *Black Banners.* See my *August Strindberg,* pp. 118–22.

27. The Swedes still celebrate a person's namesday. For example, August's day is January 7.

28. Translated in the immediately following line.

29. Cartaphilus, another name for the Wandering Jew (Ahasuerus).

30. Ahasuerus, the shoemaker in Jerusalem, according to legend, denied Christ a resting place on His way to Golgotha, and was condemned to wander throughout the world until Judgment Day.

31. I Kings 19:4.

32. The Intimate Theater (1907–10). See *The Open Letters to the Intimate Theater.*

32. Ishmael, the son of Abraham and his concubine Hagar. See Genesis 21:9 ff. for the account of their being cast out into the desert. See also Genesis 32 and 35 in which Jacob (Israel) wrestles with God.

34. See Genesis 32:26 ("I will not let thee go, except thou bless me").

Introduction to
'The Crownbride'

WHEN ROMANTICISM WAS enthusiastically renewed and developed in Sweden in the 1890s, the western province of Dalarna (literally, "the Dales" or "the Valleys") was a major source of inspiration and material. The Dalesmen were generally considered the strictest among Swedes in their faithfulness to old and traditional Swedish culture. They had retained much of the patriarchal family system, old speech patterns, traditional folkways, and such folk arts as their own style in painting (*dalmålningar*), dress, building, furniture, and folk music (fiddlers). They had, moreover, appreciably kept their centuries-old blend of provincial or regional adaptation of Christianity and pagan superstitions, and they were known nationally as well for their stubborn defense of independent ways of thinking and independent lifestyle.

In the 1890s the painters Carl Larsson (1853–1919) and Anders Zorn (1860–1920) became internationally known and appreciated at least partly because of their idyllic and moving interpretations of Dalarna and its people. Karl-Erik Forsslund (1872–1941), poet and prose writer, devoted most of his creative lifetime to interpreting and even glorifying the province and its people. Erik-Axel Karlfeldt (1864–1931), one of Sweden's many great poets, labeled many of his lyrics *dalmålningar* (literally, "Dalarna paintings"); these lyrics deal with the province and its people and are, in spirit and subject, related to the work of the many folk artists who for generations have produced wall and other paintings depicting

77

biblical characters and stories as if they were Dalesmen and Dalarna stories. There were also scores of native musicians who preserved folk music from generation to generation. Outsiders, too, found Dalarna a rich source of fascinating material. Selma Lagerlöf (1858–1940), the 1909 winner of the Nobel Prize in literature, composed *Jerusalem* (1901–2), a two-volume novel depicting the emigration of Dalesmen to Jerusalem in the late 1800s. Even before she wrote her superb interpretation, Strindberg had made his contribution to the literature about the Dalesmen with *The Crownbride* (1901).

But long before he wrote that play, he had studied the folk culture of Dalarna and used it, for example, in his cultural history, *The Swedish People on Holy Day and Everyday, in War and Peace, at Home and Abroad or A Thousand Years of the History of Swedish Culture and Manners* (1882). In 1890 he had traveled in Dalarna gathering material for articles and a possible reader about the Swedes and their land. Like most Swedes, he had been exposed very early to numerous tales about Gustav Vasa, Sweden's liberator from an unhappy union, and his adventures in sixteenth-century Dalarna. He knew very well why Dalarna has been called "the heart of Sweden," why terms like *fäbodar* ("upland farms, summer pastures"), church boats, *dalkulla* ("girl from Dalarna"), and *dalmas* or *dalkarl* ("Dalesman") had become richly connotative terms throughout Sweden, and why red-and-white cottages, white birches, and dark evergreens frequently reminded Swedes elsewhere of the western mountain province. A major result of this interest and knowledge was *Gustav Vasa* (1899), one of his finest historical dramas; among the most striking material in that play is that dealing with the Dalesmen as supporters and as opponents of the liberator-king.

A glance at the titles of the six scenes in the folk tragedy

suggests how well informed Strindberg was about Dalarna
and its ways:
    1. *The upland farm or pasture land* (grazing cattle; young
people herding, churning, cheesemaking)
    2. *The family council* (patriarchal, conservative)
    3. *The girls' get-together* (the preparation of the "virginal"
bride)
    4. *The wedding* (the procession; the postwedding
festivities: fiddlers, dancing, coffee tables)
    5. *Kersti's penance in church* (retention of centuries-old
customs)
    6. *Crossing the ice* (Lake Siljan [?], the castle = the prison
in the distance; Easter; the royal pardon; the sacrifice;
reconciliation)
    These bits of information do not suggest, however, that
The Crownbride is more than a typical sentimental folk drama.
Strindberg certainly intended, on the one hand, to write a
play that would parallel the contributions of the
contemporary artists who were capitalizing on the current
enthusiasm about folk culture. The play is, on the other
hand, subtly, yet strikingly different from the usual treatment
of the Dalesmen and their culture by outsiders. John
Landquist in his editorial notes on *The Crownbride* pointed
out the likely source of Strindberg's inspiration in Richard
Dybeck's *Svenska vallvisor och hornlåtar (Swedish Herding
Songs and Horn Melodies*, 1846). "Dybeck writes about the
motif for the song: 'a boy and a girl who were herding had a
child, which they kept in the forest in a cradle of braided
willows, which they had suspended in a birch. They took
turns looking after the child, because they were in
service.—They kept each other informed about the child's
condition, etc. in that way [i.e., by song].'" Dr. Landquist also
points out that Dybeck's couple were discovered and
forgiven.

Strindberg makes his play an in-depth examination of the crime committed by a girl theoretically trained and disciplined in the mores and practices of a folk culture. The themes are obviously Kersti's crime, Kersti's punishment, and Kersti's salvation through penitence and death. All these matters are always set against the cultural background of genuine tradition, genuine faith, and genuine practices and ways in the 1860s (during the reign of Charles XV).

Kersti appears for the first time as a lovely *dalkulla* who has made it impossible for herself to wear the bridal crown honestly. That beautiful girl is examined as a human being egotistically concerned primarily with herself and particularly in fear of what people will say and do if what she acknowledges as her sin of fornication is discovered. Note her attitudes towards Mats, her baby son, her mother, the midwife, the river sprite, and, far from least important, herself.

As Strindberg presents her, Kersti is an unhappy creature who violates one commandment after the other: fornication, false witness, cruelty to fellow beings (the river sprite and the midwife), and finally murder. Salving an increasingly sick conscience through an informal marriage ceremony, involving Mats in her ugliest sin (murder), and bargaining with the witchlike midwife do not release her from an ever-heavier burden of guilt.

What tortures her into penitence is a blend of realistic and nonrealistic matters, all of them true to her cultural background. The torture is to a great extent self-torture, which takes not only the form of pangs of conscience but reading motives into almost everything that is said to her and, what may well be even worse, imagining that supernatural forces are busy because of her sins (the child in white, the hunt, the strange phenomena in the mill). Torture comes as well, of course, steadily and cruelly, from Brita, a sister-in-law who may well be called a typical folktale in-law.

Strindberg shows how Kersti is driven inexorably to genuine penitence which culminates on her real wedding day when for the first time both reality and imagination force her to confront herself and her sins. Brought low she admits that she needs salvation and that her egotistic self is dead:

> KERSTI: I *am* dead; I have died day after day!—
>
> BRITA: You shall die still more in days to come! You shall die for perjury, for lying, for killing, for theft, for insult, for deceit! You shall die six times! And the seventh will be only for the sake of appearance!

Kersti has been brought to the point where she can accept imprisonment and church discipline without inward or outward protest and where she can refuse both a chance to escape physically and a reprieve from the king. Her death through drowning on Easter morning is the death of a chastened human being who has found inner peace in preparation for salvation in the hereafter.

All of these matters are in keeping with her cultural heritage. The biblical injunction, "The wages of sin is death," was, of course, part of her people's religious code as was the whole doctrine of salvation through penitence and acceptance of Christ through faith. Other terms—crime and punishment—can be applied equally well to this highly moving story of one promising human being who pays the penalty for not abiding by her people's—and her own—code.

The title of the play is, as usual in Strindberg's plays, significant. The only character who receives the kind of attention that Strindbergian "characterless characters" (that is, genuinely human beings, complex and dynamic beings) received in his plays which are not dream plays is, in this play, Kersti. Each of the genuinely human beings—the relatives of both Kersti and Mats, Kersti's girl friends, the pastor, the other wedding guests, and even Mats—receive only the degree of characterization needed to reveal Kersti in her complexity and her development.

The degree of characterization for many of these is sufficient to suggest that they are creatures of flesh and blood: Kersti's mother a woman who knows but hopes against hope; her father who doesn't quite rise to the occasion when needed; Mats attractive and instrumental but not really central in Kersti's life; Brita not only envious and cruel but discerning and aware; the children attractive in their innocence and insight into what is essentially good and fine in Kersti; Mats's people as practitioners of a way of life; the sheriff as the friend whose innocently intended remarks are easily misinterpreted; the pastor in his role as pastor. The rest—the fiddlers, for example, are merely human figures, essential parts of the background.

Then there are the midwife, the river sprite, and the child in white, all of them wholly or partially creatures of the imagination, real enough in terms of cultural superstitions. The tales about midwives who were not only much needed and welcome members of the community but who perhaps most of all because of their superior knowledge of life and death impressed and even terrified the folk were sometimes tales in which the midwife was transformed into a startling combination of what is human and good and what is inhuman and evil. The river sprite is, of course, a centuries-old creature of human imagination quite capable of seeing nonhuman creatures in external nature and of ascribing to them powers and roles. The child in white presents no difficulty in acceptance to a Kersti and a Brita conditioned to miracles and wonders.

The ancient theme of family feuds reminds the reader and the theatergoer of what is probably the most famous of such literary feuds, that between the Montagues and the Capulets and that led to the deaths of Romeo and Juliet. It is, however, the story of feuding on a different level and in a different environment. In Strindberg's play the participants are nineteenth-century Dalesmen behaving and speaking in their own fashion. They are decidedly individualistic functioning within a patriarchal society; they are introverted rather than extroverted; they have a strictly conservative code; they generally speak, Strindberg said, "Icelandically," that is, laconically, pithily, pointedly. Much of the dialog is therefore stylized in the sense that they use few words, mean much, and are understood by each other. Their conversation is, moreover, laced with quotations from the Bible and with folk sayings.

When Strindberg had completed *The Crownbride*, he submitted it to the Royal Opera for consideration for performance there. He wrote in a letter to his friend Emil Grandinson after the play had been rejected:

> The theater which has had room for such "whoppers" as *Cyrano*
> . . . certainly has a place for *The Crownbride* which isn't based
> on scenery but on sound ensembles, moods, and psychic and
> emotional effects. [*Strindbergs brev*, 14: Letter 4577]

Strindberg was right, of course: *The Crownbride* is essentially a lyric folk tragedy. Its use of lures, fiddles, melodies, and antiphony is undoubtedly largely responsible for highly successful productions of the play (Strindberg's daughter Greta and his third wife Harriet Bosse were among the first to create the role of Kersti, incidentally). The musical elements are undoubtedly responsible for the interest two of Sweden's leading composers have had in it: Tor Aulin (1866–1914) composed the music for its production and Ture Rangström (1864–1947) converted the play into an opera in 1918.

The Crownbride

'Characters'

MATS
KERSTI
KERSTI'S MOTHER
THE SOLDIER, *Kersti's father*
THE CHURCH CUSTODIAN (*the* VERGER), *Kersti's paternal grandfather*
BRITA, *Mats's sister*
MATS'S PATERNAL GRANDFATHER
MATS'S FATHER
MATS'S MOTHER
MATS'S PATERNAL GRANDMOTHER
ANNA, *Mats's sister*
LILL-KAREN, *Mats's sister*
LILL-MATS, *Mats's brother*
THE SHERIFF
THE PASTOR
THE RIVER SPRITE
THE MIDWIFE
THE CHILD IN WHITE
THE FISHERMAN
Minor characters

Settings

1. The upland farm
2. The family council at the mill
3. The girls' get-together at Kersti's home the night before the wedding
4. The wedding at the mill
5. Kersti's penance in church
6. Crossing the ice

Scene i

An upland summer pasture in Dalarna.[1] *In the foreground a wooden cabin painted red; next to it two birches with trunks white to their roots; to the right a fir-covered slope with a small waterfall [in a stream]; at its foot a tarn with water lilies on it. In the background a large lake with blue mountains on the distant shore. A church can be seen in the distance. A grindstone is mounted next to the cabin. It is sunset on a Sunday.*

    KERSTI'S MOTHER *is sitting on a block of wood outside the cabin smoking a pipe.*

    KERSTI *enters with her alpenhorn, or grazing lure,*[2] *in her hand and stops in front of her* MOTHER.

MOTHER: Where have you been all this time, Daughter?

KERSTI: In the forest, Mother!

MOTHER: Picking wild strawberries, I see by your red lips.

KERSTI: Why did you call me, Mother?

MOTHER: There are noises and stealthy sounds in the forest, Child. Is the bear about?

KERSTI: Can't tell!

MOTHER: Did I hear an axe or didn't I?

KERSTI: The bear doesn't have an axe, Mother.

MOTHER: Why are you dressed up, Daughter?

KERSTI: Isn't it Sunday, Mother?

MOTHER: You have milk on your bib, Child. Have you been milking May Rose or Star?

KERSTI: If I could only milk the stars—and the moon!

MOTHER: At night!

KERSTI: Day and night!

MOTHER: Night and day! . . . I know! Watch out for the bear!

KERSTI: Would he hurt our bellcow?

MOTHER: Have you lost her?

KERSTI: Shall I ask Anna?

MOTHER: Ask her!

KERSTI (*takes her lure and plays*):

(*then she sings*):

An - na in Björ - as, can you see a bit of

my cow, of my bell-cow where you are?

MATS (*answers in a clear tenor in the distance*):

Yes come here, dear! Your own cow,

your bell-cow is down here.

MOTHER: Strange how Anna's voice has changed!

KERSTI: She's been herding her cows since daybreak.

MOTHER: What do you hear from down below, Child?

KERSTI: The bellcow's bell, the goat's smaller one . . .

MOTHER: No!

KERSTI: I hear the cock crowing, the dog barking, the gun banging, the cart creaking, and the oars going "lock-lock" in the oarlocks.

MOTHER: Whose cock? Whose dog?

KERSTI: The miller's.

MOTHER: What's the miller's name?

(KERSTI *does not answer.*)

MOTHER: Is his name Anna?

(KERSTI *embarrassed, says nothing.*)

MOTHER: What do you see down there?

KERSTI: The waterwheel in the rapids, the smoke from the chimney . . .

MOTHER: Whose chimney?

(KERSTI *does not answer.*)

MOTHER: The millfolk's?

KERSTI: It's getting late, Mother!

MOTHER: I *am* going! before it gets dark! . . . (*Gets up*) This has been the longest Sunday I've lived through! . . . What's that smell?

KERSTI: The smell of woods, of cattle, of hay . . .

MOTHER: Oh no, those were tattleberries[3] you picked. (*Then becomes lost in thought. She sings*):

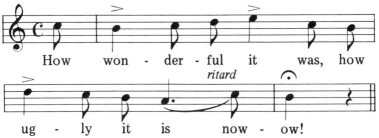

How won - der - ful it was, how
ug - ly it is now - ow!

(*Speaks*): How wonderful it was, how ugly it is now!

KERSTI: It's getting dark, Mother!

MOTHER: I see that, Daughter! The darkness falls thick as a blanket, and now I'll go down . . . down! But you stay to watch the curds![4] Be sure the smoke will tell me if the fire goes out!

KERSTI: The fire's not going to go out, trust me, Mother.

MOTHER: Good night then! Don't forget to say your evening prayer!

KERSTI: Good night, Mother!

MOTHER: "How wonderful it was, how ugly it is now!"—Don't forget your prayer! (*Goes out to the left*).

KERSTI: (*opens the door to the cabin; one can see a kettle above the fire which she shakes up; comes out and picks up the lure after she has looked to see that her* MOTHER *has gone. Plays*):

MATS (*answers, singing, from the distance to the right*):

Ker - sti dar-ling, Ker - sti dar-ling, Ba-by's sleep-ing in

the for'st.   Far,   far   off   in   the   for'st.

KERSTI (*sings*):

Did - de - ly dee! Does he still live?

Does he still live far off in the for-est?

MATS (*sings*):

In - deed he does. In - deed he does. Ba - by does

sleep in his cra-dle, far, far off in the for'st.

KERSTI (*sings*):

Take off your shoe and milk the cow and

give our ba - by some warm milk! I can-not come; I

may-n't herd cows. I'm help-ing Mo-ther with cook-ing.

MATS (*sings*):

Winds are blow-ing and birch-es sway and Ba-by's

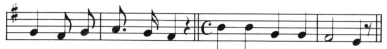

still a-sleep still a-sleep,   Ker-sti, Ker-sti dar-ling.

The wind begins to blow. The stage is in shadow, but at the very top of the evergreen forest to the right the sun is still shining. Then can be heard round about and back of the hut, first in the distance then closer at hand, shouts and cries from men beating up or starting game, branches breaking, dogs barking, horses trotting and galloping, shots, rattles, trees crashing, the ever louder sound of the waterfall. Then this canon by ten hunting horns, the first one begins and repeats while the rest join in one by one.

KERSTI *frightened, looks about; when the noises have died away in the distance, she goes into the cabin and carries out spruce twigs,[5] which she places on the ground and covers with a many-colored rug; then she puts up on each side of the door two spruce trees stripped of their bark and branches except at the tops; then she goes down to the tarn and picks white water lilies, which she binds together as a wreath for her head.*

MATS *comes in from the left with the baby in a leather cradle with straps attached.*

KERSTI (*rushes up and kisses the baby*): Baby, darling, are you still sleeping?

MATS: Of course he is!

KERSTI: Here—let the trees rock him!

(*They fasten the cradle between the two birches, which sway in the wind.*)

KERSTI (*hums*): "And the wind blows, the cradle will rock, and baby will sleep"—Mats, did you hear the hunt?

MATS: No hunting this late!

KERSTI: But I heard it!

MATS: Not really!. . . What did your mother say?

KERSTI: She tortured me as if she could torture the life out of me!

MATS: Well, Kersti darling, we'll get neither peace nor happiness before our union has been blessed and the baby baptized!

KERSTI: As long as our parents are against it, we'll get no wedding; but we'll ask God to bless our union before we give the baby a name.

MATS: That's what we've said, so let's do it now!

KERSTI: Can't you see I've everything ready?

MATS: Good that you have; poor things we are, poor wedding we get.

KERSTI: May God see in our hearts and minds we harbor no deceit. . . the rest doesn't matter! Do you have *the* Book?

MATS: Yes, I do! But I hope this isn't a sin, Kersti dear!

KERSTI: Far from it! The midwife has the right to christen him!

MATS: Yes, *she* does!

KERSTI (*puts the wreath on her head*): May we start then?

MATS: In the name of the Lord! May we never regret this.

(*They kneel directly opposite each other on the rug;* MATS *takes out a ring, which* KERSTI *takes hold of, while* MATS *reads from the psalmbook*): "I Mats Anders Larsson take you Kersti Margreta Hansdotter as my lawfully wedded wife to love for better or worse and in token thereof, I give you this ring."

KERSTI: "I Kersti Margreta Hansdotter take you Mats Anders Larsson as my lawfully wedded husband to love for better or worse, and in token thereof, I receive this ring."
(*They say a short prayer silently, get up, take each other's hands but do not kiss.*)

MATS: Well, Kersti, now you're mine in the sight of God. What people will say makes no difference to us.

KERSTI: We'll find out!

MATS: Kersti dear, what do we have to eat?

KERSTI: Not a thing, Mats!

MATS (*after a pause*): Then we'll have to smoke our pipes. (*They sit down on three-legged stools and smoke after using flint and steel to get fire.*) What did you say a bit ago about the hunt, Kersti?

KERSTI: I just can't bear any more, Mats, now that I understand what sort of folk they were.[6] I just can't!

MATS: Better not then! . . . Look at the cradle going as if it were rocking by itself!

KERSTI: It's the wind, Mats! The wind in the birches!

MATS: But there's no wind in the evergreens!

KERSTI: Well-l, there isn't! So, there's evil about tonight!

MATS: Don't say that!

KERSTI: See my smoke's going north!

MATS: And mine south!

KERSTI: And the mosquitoes are dancing . . .

MATS: As at a wedding . . .

KERSTI: Are we happier now?

MATS: Hardly!

KERSTI (*after a pause*): Can you hear the grouse calling?

MATS: As at a wedding . . .

KERSTI: But no church bell's ringing . . .

MATS: They're tired after Sunday services . . . What shall we name the baby?

KERSTI (*wildly*): Burden, Bad Luck, Hadto, Crownthief . . .

MATS: Why Crownthief?

KERSTI: Because and because and because. . . . They'll never let me wear the crown even if we get a regular wedding! What shall we call him? Bride Spoiler, Mother's Sorrow, Forest Lad!

MATS: Evil to him who evil does!

KERSTI: Really?

(MOTHER *can be seen in the forest, observing* KERSTI *and* MATS).

MATS: I can feel evil eyes on us!

KERSTI: And evil thoughts . . . you brew and I drink; you grind and I bake.

(MOTHER *disappears*).

MATS: Do you know why our families have hated each other so terribly?[7]

KERSTI: It had to do with land! With bribes and illegal gains, about a corrupt judge, and . . . everything bad, bad, bad!

MATS: And hate turned into love, desire, lust. . . .

KERSTI: But poisoned, all of it!

MATS: And dark when hate came!

KERSTI (*throws her wreath into the tarn*): You may well say that! Let the devil take the wreath when I don't get the crown . . .

MATS: Don't say that!

KERSTI: As beggars, as tramps, as swindlers, we celebrate our wedding. . . . We can't eat it, we can't drink it, but we can taste it; that's the tobacco! That's the wedding fare! The fire's going out under the kettle, get some wood, Mats! That'll be the dance!

MATS: If the signs speak the truth, you were born to be a queen!

KERSTI: Perhaps! Certainly not to milk cows!

MATS: Dear, dear! Lord, what a life!

KERSTI: Poor little thing! What's to become of us? What's

ahead of us? . . . Get some wood, Mats! The curdling will
stop, then Mother will beat me! Go on, Mats!

MATS: Kersti, you worked for my dad once; now I'm working
for you. He was strict with you; so I'll be kind!

KERSTI: You are good, Mats. I'm not! I wish I were!

MATS: Become!

KERSTI: Mats, become bad and we'll see if you can!

MATS: You don't mean that!

KERSTI: Who knows?—Hurry, Mats; someone's coming; I
know her walk; it's Mother!

MATS: Mother?—What about the baby?

KERSTI (*picks up the rug, throws it over the cradle, and then takes
her coat from the wall and spreads it over the rug*): Hurry!
Hurry!

MATS: Take care of the baby! Take care of him! (*Goes out to
the left.*)

KERSTI: Yes, yes, yes!

MOTHER (*enters from the left*): Was it Anna who was here?

KERSTI: Yes, it was!

MOTHER (*fixes* KERSTI's *gaze*): And it was she who left? . . .
And has such a deep voice?

KERSTI: Strange, isn't it?

MOTHER: And she cut the wedding poles and branches, too?

KERSTI: What's wrong with that?

MOTHER (*pulls* KERSTI's *hair*): Liar, hussy, strumpet . . .

KERSTI (*raises her hand*): Haven't you any shame?

MOTHER: Do you raise your hand against your mother, you
bitch! Was it Mats who taught you? Mats' father drove us
from our farm and home, and you take his son in your
arms, Daughter! . . . O-o!

KERSTI: O-o! for that!

MOTHER (*points at the cradle*): What do you have there?

KERSTI: I'm airing clothes!

MOTHER: Tiny clothes!

KERSTI: Not so tiny!

MOTHER: What do you have in the cradle?

KERSTI: Tiny clothes, but not too tiny.

MOTHER: It's the child!

KERSTI: Which?

MOTHER: Yours!

KERSTI: No!

MOTHER: Will you swear?

KERSTI: I swear! May the River Sprite[8] take me if I'm lying!

MOTHER: You shouldn't swear by the evil one!

KERSTI: By anyone else never!

MOTHER (*sits down*): There's talk in the village!

KERSTI: Oh!

MOTHER: Strange talk!

KERSTI: Really!

MOTHER: They say Mats is to get the mill!

KERSTI (*stands up*): Is that true?

MOTHER: As true as that an impatient spirit brings misfortune on herself!

KERSTI: So Mats is to get the mill? Then he'll marry, I suppose?

MOTHER: That's said, too!

KERSTI: With whom?

MOTHER: Who knows? the one he loves, certainly she has to be a crownbride.

KERSTI: Oh!

MOTHER: Oh!

*

MOTHER: You have a ring on your finger!

KERSTI: Yes!

MOTHER: Are you betrothed?

KERSTI: Yes!

MOTHER: But the bridal crown?

(KERSTI *remains silent*).

MOTHER: Have you lost it?

KERSTI (*walks back and forth uneasily*): Did you know the fortune teller says I'll wear a queen's crown?

MOTHER: Nonsense, talk; a virgin's crown is lovelier than a queen's! Happy the one who can wear it with honor!

KERSTI: Oh!

MOTHER: Oh!

*

MOTHER: We were poor; wicked people injured us; misfortune came upon us! Alas!

KERSTI: We were poor, we'll be rich! Fortune'll come!

MOTHER: Two families in hate; fire and water; now it's boiling!

KERSTI: The fire burned, the water doused it; now it'll get warm!

MOTHER (*gets up to go*): "How wonderful it was, how ugly it is now!" (*Goes to the right.*) There's a wreath in the water. Where's the crown? (*Exits.*)

KERSTI: It will come, it will come!

*

The RIVER SPRITE *(Näcken) can be seen in a bright white light up by the waterfall. He is dressed in a silver tunic with a bright green belt about his waist and a red cap. He has long blond hair. He is playing on a golden violin with a silver bow.*

SPRITE (*sings and plays*):

I do hope   I do hope   that my

Re-deem-er still liv-eth.

ad libitum

Violin

KERSTI (*at first has stood deep in thought; then catches sight of the*
   RIVER SPRITE, *and when he has completed the first reprise, she*
   says contemptuously): Surely you don't have any Redeemer!
   (*The* SPRITE *pauses, observes her sadly, and sings his song*
   over twice.)
KERSTI: If you keep still now, you may play at my wedding!
   (*The* SPRITE *nods assent and the cliff encloses him.*)
MIDWIFE (*enters from in back of the shed, clad in a long black*
   circular cloak and a black hood. Under her cloak she is carrying
   a bag. She does not turn her back to the audience): Good
   evening, dear girl! My coming's not inconvenient, I hope!
KERSTI: Oh, it's the midwife, Mrs. Larsson?
MIDWIFE: Of course it is! Why, I'm the one who helped you,
   dear . . .
KERSTI: Yes, yes, but you promised never to say anything
   about that!
MIDWIFE: And we won't talk about *that*! But . . . how is the
   baby?
KERSTI (*impatient*): He's all right!
MIDWIFE: Listen, dear, don't get impatient . . .
KERSTI: Who said I am?
MIDWIFE: Your voice and your foot, dear! . . . But you have
   a ring on your finger, I see. So I'll get to go to the wedding
   soon?
KERSTI: You?
MIDWIFE: I'm always at christenings, of course, but I've never
   been at a wedding. . . . I think that would be fun!
KERSTI: I bet you do!
MIDWIFE: Of all human virtues there is one I value most . . .
KERSTI: That can't be chastity!

MIDWIFE: What doesn't exist can't be valued. But gratitude, see, that I do value!

KERSTI: Were you paid?

MIDWIFE: There are favors that can't be paid for with money!

KERSTI: And people who never think they've really been paid.

MIDWIFE: Absolutely right, dear; and that's the kind I belong to . . .

KERSTI: I've noticed that!

MIDWIFE: I . . . and one other person!

KERSTI: Who?

MIDWIFE: The sheriff!

KERSTI (*taken aback*): The sheriff?

MIDWIFE: Yes! The sheriff! He's a really remarkable man, and I know no one who knows the law by heart from cover to cover as he does. . . . You and I'd never be able to learn it as well as he! But . . . there is one chapter, which I as midwife have to know by heart . . . that's the remarkable fourteenth chapter; it's *too* remarkable with its many paragraphs. . . . What's the matter?

KERSTI (*shaken*): Say what you know!

MIDWIFE: I know nothing at all. . . . I'm only a poor old woman who needs to stay here overnight. . . .

KERSTI: Here? Stay here?

MIDWIFE: Right here!

KERSTI: Be off!

MIDWIFE: I can't walk in the forest in the darkness of night . . .

KERSTI (*picks up a stick and threatens her*): Then you'll get to run in there!

MIDWIFE (*draws back a little without turning around*): So that's it, so that's it now! Drop the stick, or . . .

KERSTI: Or?

MIDWIFE: It'll be the sheriff, of course! And the fourteenth chapter. . .

KERSTI (*lifts the stick to strike her*): Go to hell, you damned witch! (*The stick goes to pieces.*)

(*The* MIDWIFE *laughs.*)

KERSTI (*takes up flint and steel and strikes fire*): In the name of Christ's suffering, get thee hence!

MIDWIFE (*turns so one can see a foxlike back and tail; she flees in a gallop, hissing*): We'll meet at the wedding, invited, uninvited! With the sheriff! With the sheriff! (*Hisses*).

*

(KERSTI *alone; first at a loss, goes to the tarn as if she wanted to throw herself in; then walks back and forth in front of the cradle; then she takes off her sweater and lays it on top of the other things in the cradle. Then she sits down on the chair by the door; covers her face with her hands.*)

(*Now the grindstone begins to turn and make a hissing noise; then the pingling of small bells like the goats'; small bright lights appear in the evergreen forest; and cowbells nearby can be heard; then the* RIVER SPRITE *appears and repeats his refrain*):

"I do hope, I do hope, that
my Redeemer still liveth."

(KERSTI *has risen and stands as if turned to stone by horror.*)

(*From the tarn can now be heard sounds as if from a glass-harmonica; a* CHILD *clad in white and unseen by* KERSTI *rises among the lilies in the tarn, goes up to the cradle; it becomes silent on stage; the grindstone stops. The* RIVER SPRITE *disappears, all but one of the bright lights die out. The* CHILD IN WHITE, *still unseen by* KERSTI, *touches the cradle gently, listens, and seems very sad. He begins to cry and covers his face with his sleeve. The harmonica can still be heard. Then the* CHILD *picks lilies to pieces so that the petals fall on the cradle, kisses it, and goes down into the tarn again. The last light goes out, and the harmonica quits playing.*)

*

MIDWIFE (*reenters carrying her bag*): Maybe I may come now?
Maybe you'll receive the midwife now!
KERSTI: What do you offer?
MIDWIFE (*takes a bridal crown from her bag*): This! . . .
KERSTI: What will you take?
MIDWIFE (*pointing at the cradle*): You see it, I see it, the whole
world sees it, and yet it doesn't exist!
KERSTI: Then take it!
MIDWIFE (*goes up to the cradle*): I have it! (*She takes something
stealthily out of the cradle, puts it into her bag, and then hides
the bag under her cloak.*) May I come to the wedding, then?
KERSTI: Come!
MIDWIFE: Say "Welcome!"
KERSTI: Then I'd be lying!
MIDWIFE: Practice . . .
KERSTI: You will be welcome . . . if you leave now!
       (*The* MIDWIFE *withdraws backwards, muttering some charm
or other.*)   *

MATS (*sings offstage, jubilantly*):

Come dar - ling dar - ling   dar - ling, come dar - ling

dar - ling.

       (KERSTI *listens, happy, swelling with pride and courage.*)
       (MATS *enters with an armful of wood; happy.*)
KERSTI (*going up to him*): Did you meet anyone?
MATS: My yes! . . . There's going to be a wedding. (*Throws*

the wood down in the cabin.) Let the kettle boil over, I'm boiling, too!

KERSTI: Was it your father?

MATS: Father and Mother! And I get the mill!

KERSTI (*shows him the crown*): Do you see what I—

MATS: Where did you get it?

KERSTI: My mother gave it to me!

MATS: Was she here?

KERSTI: *She* was glad!

MATS: But the baby, the baby!

KERSTI: Sit down, Mats! Sit down! I'm not helpless!

MATS (*sits down*): The baby, the baby!

KERSTI: There!—Mats! Now that our worries can be over and life be good, don't you think we can with patience go a long ways—

MATS: But straight and direct—

KERSTI: Of course, straight and direct!

MATS: What do you have in mind?

KERSTI: To get what's big, the little has to be rejected!

MATS: Have you learned to speak plainly?

KERSTI: Wait!

MATS: I'm waiting!

KERSTI: Your parents have set conditions!

MATS: I know!

KERSTI: They insist on a crownbride? What's a crownbride? The one who wears the crown!

MATS: With honor!

KERSTI: With or without! What doesn't show, what no one knows, doesn't exist!

MATS: Let me think! (*He thinks.*) Well, yes! But then?

KERSTI: One gets what's big, if one rejects what's little!

MATS: But not *the* little one!

KERSTI: Are you going to let me down?

MATS: I won't! I won't let you down, Kersti dear!

KERSTI: We'll say: The bans have been published, the wedding prepared, but the baby sleeps in the forest. Who milks the cow? Who will pour milk into his shoe for our child? Who, who, who?

MATS: You may well ask! (*Thinks.*) If we dared. . . . Did you say something?

KERSTI: Not a thing.

MATS: I thought you did!—If we dared. . . .

KERSTI: Say it!

MATS: No, you say it!

KERSTI: No, you!

MATS: Someone has to look after the baby!

KERSTI: Who?

MATS: There's only one!

KERSTI: That's easy to guess!

MATS: Say it then!

KERSTI: No, you say it!

MATS: There's only one, besides us, who knows about the baby!

KERSTI: Who?

MATS: Since you know, why don't you say it?

KERSTI: Because you're to say it!

MATS: The midwife! Isn't that what you said?

KERSTI: I didn't say anything, but you did!—And I'll obey you, Mats; you know that!

MATS: I wonder!

KERSTI: But I already have! The baby mustn't be in the forest, must be indoors, there'll be cold nights, and if something happens, the sheriff—will come!

MATS: The sheriff! Yes, he'll come!

KERSTI (*springs to her feet*): Is the sheriff coming?

MATS: If something happens!—well then, where is the midwife?

KERSTI: Will you call her?

MATS: I wish she were here!

KERSTI: What do you want of her?

MATS: That she'd bring the baby indoors!

KERSTI: Where?

MATS: Her place!

KERSTI: For how long?

MATS: Until the wedding's over!

KERSTI: But if he gets sick?

MATS: Rather that than his freezing in the forest. (*Listening toward the cradle.*) Sh-h! I heard him!

KERSTI: No! He's sleeping—

MATS: Sh-h, I heard him!

KERSTI: No, you didn't!

MATS (*gets up*): Sh-h, I heard him!

KERSTI (*places herself in front of the cradle*): Don't wake him up! If he cries, someone may hear him.

MATS: Oh!—Do you think someone has heard him? That your mother has heard him!—We should never have done this, Kersti, dear!

KERSTI: It'd be best undone!

MATS (*sadly*): We'll have to bring him to the midwife tonight! I have to go to the village!

KERSTI: I'll take him to her!

MATS (*approaches the cradle*): You take him!

KERSTI: But don't wake him up!

MATS: But I may surely say good-night to him!

KERSTI: Don't touch him!

MATS: Think of it—if I never got to see him again!

KERSTI: Then the will of Him we can't change would be done!

MATS: Let His will be done!

KERSTI: You did say it!

MATS: What did I say that pleases you so?

KERSTI: That, that—you bend before His will, without which nothing can be done!

MATS (*naïvely*): Surely, everything that happens is His will—

KERSTI: Surely!

MATS: Good-night then, Kersti dear, and little one! (*Goes.*)

KERSTI: Good-night, Mats!

*

(KERSTI *takes the empty cradle and sinks it in the tarn. The* CHILD IN WHITE *rises and shakes his finger threateningly.* KERSTI *shrinks back.*)

RIVER SPRITE (*appears again, threatening, now with a golden harp and bare-headed, and sings as he accompanies himself on the harp*):

The clouds pass on, the waters stand still,
the waters stand still;
I saw the sun, when in the dawn of time
I was blessed;
the sun has set,
the night is near;
the sin is heavy,
the stream is deep.
Bright it was then!
Black it is now!
In the World of Endless Anguish I dwell!
Oh!

In the meanwhile KERSTI *has taken the bridal crown and carried it into the cabin; when she then puts out the fire under the kettle, smoke rises from the chimney and on the smoke can be seen fantastically shaped and many colored snakes, dragons, birds, etc.*

When she comes out, she is wearing a sweater, has a bag at her side and a lure in her hand. She shuts the door, locks it, and walks away, erect with proud steps just as the RIVER SPRITE *sings his last verse.*

[CURTAIN]

SCENE 2

*The living room in the mill. Everything is white from flour.
At the back to the right is a large open trapdoor through which
one can see part of the waterwheel; a little to the right, the end
of the chute with a flour sack attached to its end; next to it, the
control lever. At the back center are large gates; to the left of
these, large shutters as in a barn.*

*To the front right is a large open fireplace in which a coal fire
is burning and over which a kettle is suspended. To the left are
a bed and a loom, a bobbin, a reel, and a spinning wheel. A door
is to the right.*

Sitting in a circle in front of the fireplace: MATS'S
GRANDFATHER, GRANDMOTHER, MOTHER *and* FATHER,
BRITA *(Mats's older sister),* ANNA *(Mats's teenage sister),*
LILL-KAREN *(his sister, a child),* LILL-MATS *(his brother, a
child). All are smoking small iron pipes and are very serious.*
BRITA *is busy creating something with hair.* LILL-KAREN *and*
LILL-MATS *each hold a doll.*[9]

BRITA (*to* LILL-KAREN): Where did you take that doll?

LILL-KAREN: Kersti gave it to me!

BRITA (*takes the doll away from her*): Throw it away! . . . (*to*
LILL-MATS)
Where did you take that doll?

LILL-MATS: Kersti gave it to me!

BRITA (*takes his doll*): Away with it!

FATHER: Sh-h! Sh-h! Grandfather's thinking! (*Silence.*)

MOTHER (*to* BRITA): What are you making?

BRITA: It's a watchchain, but I'm almost out of hair.

MOTHER: Where can you get any?

BRITA: I certainly know where I ought to pull it out!

MOTHER: Horses' manes are pulled.

BRITA: And hens are plucked, sows give up bristles, and girls
    are combed! Combed out hair is fine, but clipped is best!
FATHER: Sh-h, sh-h, Grandfather's thinking! (*Silence.*)
ANNA (*softly to* BRITA): What is he thinking about?
BRITA: You'll find out! And we'll have to put up with it!
ANNA: Is it about Mats?
    (BRITA *does not answer.*)
ANNA: And Kersti? Is there going to be a wedding?
FATHER: Sh-h! Sh-h! Grandfather's thinking! (*Silence.*)
ANNA (*to* BRITA): You may have some of my hair!
BRITA: Yours isn't the right color!
ANNA: Whose is?
    (BRITA *does not answer.*)
ANNA: Kersti's?
BRITA: Don't mention *her*! (*Silence.*)
GRANDMOTHER (*to* GRANDFATHER): Have you thought?
GRANDFATHER (*with a Bible and a psalmbook or hymnal on his
    lap, deep in thought, wakes up*): I have thought! (*Opens the
    psalmbook at random; says to the others*) Number 278 and
    Stanza 4, "Death and Birth," we'll take that one! [10]
ALL (*read in unison as children in school*):
    "Death and birth make us equal,
    as the bones of dead men tell,
    then try to sort rich from poor,
    who was less from who was more.
    Seek the cradle, see and learn
    if in that child you can discern
    the one with gifts and gold
    revealed in innocence untold."
GRANDFATHER: It is said! He who has ears to hear, let him
    hear!—Is it said?
GRANDMOTHER: Not yet.
FATHER: Not quite.

MOTHER: Lord Jesus, You see it!

BRITA: What do the Scriptures say?

ANNA: "Doth God pervert judgment? or doth the Almighty pervert justice?"[11]

LILL-KAREN: What shall I say?

GRANDFATHER: Well, my child, you may advise us, even though we do not obey; the truth can be heard from the mouths of babes. . . . Is Kersti to get Mats?

LILL-KAREN: If they want each other!

GRANDFATHER: Well said! (*then to* LILL-MATS) Lill-Mats!

LILL-MATS (*fingers in his mouth*): I want my doll!

GRANDFATHER: And Mats wants his! Should he?

LILL-MATS: If it's Kersti, he may, for she's the one who gave me my doll.

BRITA: Listen to that!

GRANDFATHER: Let us go to the Scriptures! (*Opens the Bible at random and reads.*) Genesis, Chapter 3, verse 8: "And Hamor communed with them, saying, The soul of my son Shechem longeth for your daughter: I pray you give her him to wife." Is that enough?

GRANDMOTHER: Enough for God!

FATHER: Did it say something about the mill, too?

MOTHER: His will be done!

BRITA (*sharply*): Amen.

ANNA: Yes, yes, it shall so be done!

LILL-KAREN: I like Kersti because she's kind.

LILL-MATS: I do, too!

FATHER: Sh-h, sh-h! Grandfather's thinking! (*Silence.*)

GRANDFATHER (*to the* FATHER): Call in Brother-in-law!

    (FATHER *gets up and goes to the door at the back, where he stops.*)

GRANDFATHER (*goes to the bed, pulls out a drawer under it, and takes out a bundle of legal documents. Turns to the* FATHER): Let him come!

FATHER (*opens the door*): In here, Stig Matsson, my brother-in-law!

                                     *

SHERIFF (*in uniform, enters*): Bless this house!

ALL (*rise*): Bless you!

GRANDFATHER: Stig Matsson! I have asked you to come; you know why! Kersti Margreta Hansdotter—(*Sighs*)— is to be married by Mats Anders Larsson, my grandson! The families have feuded and fought for a long time, entirely too long; I have at long last understood that before I close my eyes and go to my final rest, there has to be an end to quarreling and squabbling! Take a look at these papers. . . . (*The* SHERIFF *takes the papers and looks through them.*) They are court proceedings, distributions of inheritances, wills and testaments, receipts, powers of attorney, some concerning settled cases, some still unsettled. Have you looked through them?

SHERIFF: I have!

GRANDFATHER (*takes the papers again*): Fine! Then I'll put them on the fire!—There is a time for hate, there is a time for love![12] The time for hate has to be over. . . . I long for peace—therefore I ask my nearest and dearest and my kindred to consider everything which has been as if it had never taken place—and I ask you, will you forget everything and without ill feeling or secret reservations meet your new kinsmen and greet them as friends? Answer me!

ALL: Yes!

GRANDFATHER: Then I give the evil past to the fire! (*Throws the papers on the fire, opens the damper and the small ventilators*) Let us sit down!

     (ALL *sit down about the open fire and look at its red glow which shows through the ventilators.*)

ANNA (*softly to* BRITA): Listen, it's singing!

BRITA: It's moaning!—It breaks my heart! (*Silence.*)

(GRANDFATHER *rises.*)

(ALL *rise.*)

GRANDFATHER (*to the* FATHER): Bring them in!

(FATHER *goes to the door at the right and brings in* MATS.)

(MOTHER *to the back, lets in* KERSTI, KERSTI'S MOTHER, KERSTI'S FATHER, *the* SOLDIER, *who is dressed in parade uniform,*[13] *and Kersti's grandfather, the* VERGER, *or church custodian.*)

GRANDFATHER (*with simple dignity*): God bless you!—and do sit down!

(*All sit down except* MATS *and* KERSTI *and the* SHERIFF. MATS *is holding* KERSTI'*s hands.*)

(*Silence.*)

GRANDFATHER: When do you want the wedding?

MATS: In two weeks on the third reading of the bans!

GRANDFATHER: Is there any hurry?

(KERSTI *disturbed*).

MATS: Haven't we waited long enough?

GRANDFATHER: Perhaps so!

MATS (*to his relatives*): Does no one have a word for Kersti? (*Silence.*) No one?

*

SHERIFF (*comes up to* KERSTI *and takes both her hands in friendly fashion*): So here is the child!

(KERSTI *shrinks in horror and tries to release her hands.*)

SHERIFF: Afraid of me!—Surely not!—Look me in the eyes, Kersti! I held you on my lap when you were a child, and I have had your beautiful head between my hands . . . you have such a beautiful head with a stubborn little forehead; that's why you have got what you wanted! . . . (*Releases her.*)

GRANDFATHER: Let us go and leave the young couple alone!

(ALL *get up and go by* MATS *and* KERSTI *through the door at the back.*)

BRITA (*who goes last, spits as she passes* KERSTI): Ugh!

MATS (*spits back at her*): Ugh!

*

(KERSTI *and* MATS *are alone.*)

MATS: I bid you welcome, Kersti!

KERSTI: You? Yes!

MATS: Do the others really matter?

KERSTI: That's easy to say!

MATS: Do you intend to marry the family?

KERSTI: Into the family!

MATS: Our people aren't soft, you know! and don't show they're affectionate either.[14]

KERSTI: That's easy to see . . . Is this where we're going to live?

MATS: Yes, how does it look?

KERSTI: Everything's white . . .

MATS: That's the flour! Won't it do?

KERSTI: And wet . . .

MATS: That's the water . . .

KERSTI: Cold, too!

MATS: It's below the lake!

KERSTI: Will we get new furniture?

MATS: No, indeed! Nothing new's made here! Everything's handed down!

KERSTI: May we sweep up the white stuff?

MATS: No, indeed! It's to be like that in the mill as the caking in a pipe! Mustn't be touched!

KERSTI: Is that the wheel?

MATS: That's the wheel!

(*Pulls at the lever; the water rushes, the wheel turns.*)

KERSTI: Ugh, no! Can one hear it?

MATS: It's ours! And one's thankful as long as one hears it, for then one gets flour!

KERSTI: The sun'll never shine here!

MATS: Never! How could it?

KERSTI: And nothing grows; only green slime on the wheel!

MATS: We catch eels there! and lampreys!

KERSTI: Ugh, no! It's nicer on the uplands where the wind blows. . .

MATS: And the birches rock!

KERSTI (*weeping, her apron to her eyes*): Am I to live here, below the water, on the bottom of the lake!

MATS: I was born here!

KERSTI: And we're to die here! (*Sighs with despair*)

MATS: Why that sigh?

KERSTI: Stop the wheel, then!

MATS: If you can't stand the wheel. . . well then. . .

KERSTI (*lifts a trapdoor on the floor*): What's down here?

MATS: That's the stream!

KERSTI: Stop the wheel!

MATS (*pulls at the lever, but the wheel does not stop*): Well-l! Is evil about?. . . It doesn't stop!¹⁵

KERSTI: I'll die here!

MATS: I'll go out on the footbridge and shut it off! There *is* evil about!

KERSTI: In here, too!

MATS: Kersti dear.

KERSTI: Meow, meow, said the cat!

MATS: What's that?

KERSTI: I got what I wanted!

MATS: And it wasn't worth having! (*The wheel thunders and begins to go backwards.*) Help, Lord Jesus, the wheel's going backwards! (*Goes out at the back.*)

*

(KERSTI *alone. Now the loom begins to go; the reel, the bobbin, and the spinning wheel begin to turn; the stage is lighted as if by bright sunshine; then it darkens, and the open fireplace-stove swings out on stage and back so the red glow from the three vents seem to stare at* KERSTI *while the stove pursues her. The stove returns to its place; the millwheel thunders and the* RIVER SPRITE *can be seen in the wheel with his golden violin and red cap. He sings and plays as before.*)

RIVER SPRITE:
"I do hope, I do hope,
that my Redeemer still liveth."
(*Several times.*)

KERSTI (*rushes out at the back*): Mats! Mats!
(*The* RIVER SPRITE *disappears, but the song dies away slowly.*)

*

MIDWIFE (*enters; goes up to a trapdoor in the floor, opens the door, and puts a leather bag down into it*):
If you walk again, it won't go!
If you don't walk again, it will go!
There, that's that! Now I may dance at the wedding!
(*She dances without turning her back to the audience. The loom strikes three-quarter time, the bobbin, the reel, and the spinning wheel whirl. Then she disappears out through the door at the back and when she turns her back to the audience her foxtail can be seen. The loom continues to weave, the bobbin, the reel, and the spinning wheel go on whirling.*)
(KERSTI *enters; everything stops.*)

*

(*The* VERGER *enters.*)
KERSTI: Grandfather?
VERGER: Yes, Child, I forgot something! (*Takes his large leather bag from the bed.*)

KERSTI: What do you have in that?

VERGER: Well, I just came from the sacristy . . . and am taking the numbers home to clean them . . .

KERSTI: What numbers?

VERGER: Why, the numbers I put up the hymns with, on the board . . .

KERSTI: May I see?

VERGER (*takes out the board with the brass numbers*): See, Child! . . . What's wrong, dear?

KERSTI: I don't know, Grandfather! . . . But I think I should never have come here!

VERGER: How you talk, Child!

KERSTI: There's evil in this house . . .

VERGER: Oh, no, preserve us . . . dear . . .

KERSTI (*shuddering*): Something strange has just come in . . .

VERGER: Kersti, what's going to come of this?

KERSTI: Yes, who knows, who knows!

VERGER: I have to go, my child; I have to go to the church to get the bridal crown for it's to go to the goldsmith and be polished with cream of tartar.

KERSTI: Go ahead, Grandfather . . .

GRANDFATHER: It's for your sake, you see, the crown's to be polished . . . for your sake . . . (*Goes out at the back.*)
(*The* SOLDIER *enters.*)

KERSTI: Dad?

SOLDIER: Yes, it's only me; I was going to get my helmet—I forgot it this morning! (*Takes his helmet down.*)

KERSTI: Dad, Dad, I'm terribly unhappy . . .

SOLDIER (*dryly*): What's happened?

KERSTI: Nothing!

SOLDIER: Then how can you be unhappy?

KERSTI: He doesn't understand me!

SOLDIER (*curtly while he buckles the helmet strap*): Take it easy, Child!

KERSTI: Don't go, Dad!

SOLDIER: Troubles in love soon pass—Take it easy, that's my advice! Take it easy! (*Goes.*)

*

(BRITA *enters.*)

KERSTI: What did *you* forget?

BRITA: I don't forget!

KERSTI: What are you looking for?

BRITA: You!

KERSTI: How nice!

BRITA: I wonder!

KERSTI: Hater!

BRITA: Bitch!

KERSTI: Sister-in-law!

BRITA: What's that?

KERSTI: Are you telling my fortune, you troll?

BRITA: Yes—the rope!

KERSTI: In a hanged man's house!

BRITA (*goes up to the sack which hangs by the chute*): Look, I'll tell your fortune!. . . . The mill is yours, the grist too.
(*She takes up a handful of black soil out of the sack and constructs a little grave mound on the floor with it.*):
"For their men
flighty women
ground soil
for food."[16]

KERSTI: You are a troll!

BRITA: Yes! And I can find treasures!. . . . Let me find a little treasure for you!

KERSTI: Troll, for shame; take care: You're committing a mortal sin! You'd burn in fire, you'd float on water!

BRITA (*takes a pinch of soil from the sack and strews it on*
KERSTI's *head*): I consecrate you to the dust, I crown you
with the crown of dust, may shame take you!

KERSTI: Shame, shame on you!

*

CHILD'S VOICE (*repeats*): Shame on you!

KERSTI: Who was that?

CHILD'S VOICE: Who was that?

BRITA: Guess!. . . That was the Mocker![17]

CHILD'S VOICE: The Mocker!

BRITA: The treasure is the Mocker! Do you know the
Murdered Child?

KERSTI: The Mocker? What do I have to do with him?

CHILD'S VOICE: I with him!

BRITA: The wages of sin is death!

KERSTI (*calls loudly*): Mats!

CHILD'S VOICE: Mats.

KERSTI (*sobs with despair. Loosens her red garter and ties it about
her throat*): I want to die, I want to die!

BRITA: You will, you will!

KERSTI: Hang me in a tree!

CHILD'S VOICE: In a tree!

BRITA: Not I!

MATS (*sings, outside*): "Kersti dear, is he sleeping still!"

BRITA: Far away in the forest! . . . Ugh! (*Spits it out and
leaves*).

*

MATS (*enters, happy*): Far, far away in the forest! (*Comes up in
back of* KERSTI *and puts his hands over her eyes . . .*) Who am
I?

KERSTI: You're hurting me!

MATS (*takes hold of the garter* KERSTI *stills has about her throat*):
What a necklace.

KERSTI: Let go!

MATS (*playfully pulls at the garter*): Now I'll lead you, now you're my captive, my dove, my goat that I'm to lead to pasture. (*Leads her by the garter.*) My little white kid, my lead cow! (*Sings*)

> Come bossy, bossy, bossy!
> Come bossy, bossy!

KERSTI: You are happy, Mats!

MATS: Very happy! Guess why!

KERSTI: Can't any more!

MATS: I met the midwife! . . . She had greetings from our baby.

KERSTI: No?

MATS: Yes. . . . He's sleeping, she said, very nicely, very nicely!

(KERSTI *sighs.*)

MATS: Far away in the forest! . . . What's that on your hair?

KERSTI: Dust!

MATS: Are you buried!

KERSTI: Already buried!

MATS (*brushing the dust out of her hair*): Ugh! Who did it?

KERSTI: Can't you guess?

MATS: Brita! With her evil eye!

KERSTI: Can you blind it?

MATS: Not I! Only Jesus Christ! (*The evening bell tolls.*)

KERSTI: Pray for me!

MATS: One should do that for oneself!

KERSTI: If one can!

MATS: One can when one's conscience is clear!

KERSTI: *When* is that?

MATS: Do you hear the evening bell?

KERSTI: No!

MATS: I hear it! Then you must hear it!

KERSTI (*sighs*): I don't hear it! (*Sighs with despair.*)

MATS: That *is* bad! . . . Do you hear the rapids?

KERSTI: The rapids in the forest, the flail in the barn, the cowbell on the uplands, but not the church bell!

MATS: That is bad! I remember . . . that at the old sheriff's funeral all the churchbells rang, we saw them move, but no one heard them! That is bad!

KERSTI: Brita has bewitched me!

MATS: Then she'll suffer for it!

KERSTI: Go with me to the uplands! I must see the sun!

MATS: I'll go along! . . . Kersti dear!

(KERSTI *sighs.*)

(MATS *embraces her and presses her head to his chest.*)

[CURTAIN]

SCENE 3

INTERLUDE

Virgin's Eve {girls' get-together}[18] *at* KERSTI'*s parental home. The* SOLDIER'*s cottage: over the door at the back a tin plate with his number and {Dalarna's} coat of arms; to the left and right of that door a window with flowers, the floor of heavy boards with nailheads showing, newly scrubbed.*

To the left a big open fireplace-stove with a hood. In front of it a bench covered by a woven runner. To the right under the window a bureau with an upright mirror covered by a white veil, candlesticks, plaster figures, and other little ornaments. To the front right a table with a bench. On the wall above the bench hangs the old musket with its yellow-stained birch stock,

*red sling, and percussion lock; there are also a cartridge case, a
white shoulder strap with bayonet, and a spiked helmet. Below
all these is a portrait of King Carl XV (1859–72) in full
uniform.*[19] *Through the open door at the back can be seen an
August landscape with shocks of grain.*

When the curtain goes up, the HIRED GIRL *is standing by the
open stove polishing cups, pans, kettles, and coffeepots.*

At the table to the right the VERGER *sits polishing the
numbers for the psalmboard, which lies beside the numbers. On
the table the collection bags of red velvet with silver embroidery
and tiny bells.*

The SOLDIER *in fatigue uniform and with his cap on is
sitting at the same table going through papers and making
notes with a lead pencil, which he now and then sticks in his
mouth.*

LILL-KAREN *and* LILL-MATS *are standing watching with
intense concentration what the* VERGER *is doing, their heads
resting on the edge of the table, their eyes big and fingers in their
mouths. Now and then the* VERGER *smiles at them and pats
their heads.*

KERSTI'S MOTHER *is standing by the stove holding two hand
towels up to the fire to dry.*

*When the curtain goes up, girls can be heard singing outside.
But there is a depressed mood inside and every adult is busy
with what he is doing and pays no attention to the others.*

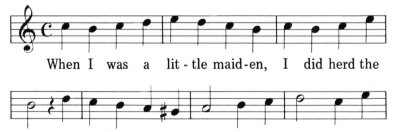

When I was a lit-tle maid-en, I did herd the

cows. Then I lost both my bell-cow and my White Star,

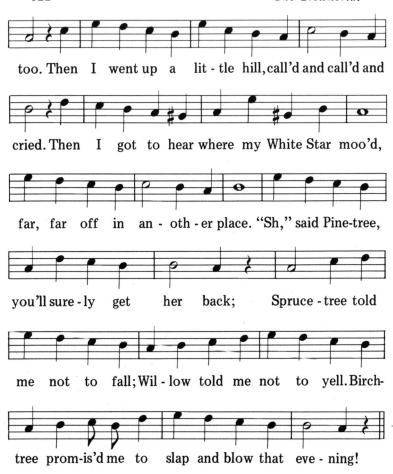

too. Then I went up a lit - tle hill, call'd and call'd and

cried. Then I got to hear where my White Star moo'd,

far, far off in an - oth - er place. "Sh," said Pine-tree,

you'll sure - ly get her back; Spruce - tree told

me not to fall; Wil - low told me not to yell. Birch-

tree prom-is'd me to slap and blow that eve - ning!

The song ends.

SOLDIER (*looks up; slowly to* MOTHER): Say, Mother!

MOTHER: Yes?

SOLDIER: Was it six barrels we got on the field last year?

MOTHER: Yes, it was six!

SOLDIER (*writing*): Fine! (*Silence.*)

VERGER: Are the girls still in the sauna?

MOTHER: Yes!—This wedding's hard on people—We should have harvested the oats—and it'll soon be time for picking lingon!

VERGER: Dog days'll soon be over; you can tell on the flies, they're sort of dazed—there'll be a lot of lingon this year!

MOTHER: Yes! (*Silence.*)

SOLDIER: Aren't the girls coming soon?

MOTHER: I don't know why they're taking so long!

SOLDIER: It is warm!

VERGER: It's not too easy for those out on maneuvers![20]

SOLDIER: I suppose it's not too bad for the infantry—

VERGER: Your getting leave was sort of lucky—

SOLDIER: It certainly was!

MOTHER: Well, they're coming now!

SOLDIER: Have you served them anything?

MOTHER: Yes, in the sauna, and plenty, too. (*Silence.*)

Talking outside can be heard; then KERSTI *comes from the sauna, pale, white-faced with hanging wet hair, followed by* BRITA *and* ANNA *and the {bridal} attendants (*ELSA, RIKEN, GRETA, LISA*). The latter four are carrying jugs and wineglasses that they place by the stove;* KERSTI, BRITA, *and* ANNA *are carrying towels with colored borders and hang them by the door.*

The MOTHER *places a chair in the middle of the room for* KERSTI, *dries her hair with towels, and then combs it. The attendants sit down on the bench to the left,* BRITA *so that she can stare at* KERSTI.

No one says anything or gives any indication of being upset.

MOTHER: Bring the mirror!

KERSTI: I don't want any mirror! Let it be!

BRITA: You ought to see yourself when no one else got to!

KERSTI: What do you mean?

BRITA: Yes, what!—beautiful hair. May I have what's combed out?

KERSTI: No!

MOTHER (*to* BRITA): What would you use it for?

BRITA: A watchchain for Mats!

MOTHER: Surely Mats may have it!

KERSTI: I don't want to!

BRITA (*takes the unfinished hairchain from her pocket*): I'll never get that color!

KERSTI: When I'm dead, you'll get it!

BRITA: See you keep your word!

KERSTI: I will! (*Silence.*)

SOLDIER: Can you tell me, Mother—be quiet, children!—if the warrant officer has been invited?

MOTHER: Vesterlund? Yes!

SOLDIER: Four o'clock tomorrow at the church, isn't that right?

MOTHER: Yes, of course!

SOLDIER (*puts his papers together*): Then I'll go to the pastor!—and then to the organist—(*To himself*)—Yes, yes—*that's that!*—*that* is *that!* (*Goes out deep in thought without saying good-bye.*)
(*Silence.*)

VERGER (*to* LILL-KAREN *and* LILL-MATS *in a friendly way*): You won't touch anything, youngsters, will you, if I go out?

LILL-KAREN: I'll see to it Lill-Mats doesn't touch anything!

VERGER: You do that!

MOTHER: Where are you going, Father?

VERGER: I'm only going to fetch the crown from the storekeeper—he's just back from town!

BRITA: Huh! the crown!

VERGER (*gets up*): The goldsmith has been polishing it with cream of tartar, you see; they clean it with tartar, the silver, I mean.

BRITA (*sneers*): Huh!

MOTHER (*to* VERGER): Wait, I'll go along to the store!

VERGER: Can we leave these youngsters alone?

BRITA: What could happen?

MOTHER: Why, they're grown-up people!

BRITA: And Kersti prefers to be alone; she can't stand anyone's looking at her—

MOTHER: Why don't you hush?

BRITA: Especially when she's in the sauna, she doesn't want any company! But she's grown up, so she isn't afraid—

(KERSTI *twists away from* BRITA's *staring.*)

MOTHER: Sit still!

BRITA: She isn't a child any more! Grown out of her childhood shoes and other things, too. Maybe the crown won't fit either. Have you tried it?

VERGER (*simply*): We're going to! (*Goes accompanied by the* MOTHER.)

(*Silence.*)

(KERSTI *sits down at the table to the right and fingers the numbers.*)

BRITA (*staring at* KERSTI): This Virgin's Eve *is* fun!

KERSTI: Do you want to play games?

BRITA: Papa and mama and the children?

KERSTI: Guess riddles?

BRITA: I've already guessed—

KERSTI: Sing?

BRITA: Lullaby, baby?—No, let's read in the Bible.

KERSTI: The Bible?

BRITA: Yes, Genesis, thirty-fourth and eighth.[21]

KERSTI: About Shechem.

BRITA: Yes, that's it! And about Dina that his heart longed for—. Do you know *who* Dina was?

KERSTI: She was Jacob's and Leah's daughter!

BRITA: Right!—Do you know *what* she was?

KERSTI: Is that a riddle?

BRITA: Oh no!—Do you know *what* she was?

KERSTI: No!

BRITA: She was a little de—spoiled!

KERSTI: Is this a word game?

BRITA: Absolutely!

(KERSTI *lowers her head as if she wanted to conceal it.*)

BRITA: Do you get it?

(*Silence.*)

BRITA: Have you invited others besides Madam Larsson?

KERSTI: Have I invited—? The midwife?

BRITA: Well, she said you had!

KERSTI: Then she lied.

BRITA: She's under oath as midwife; but if her oath's kept or not I can't say. She doesn't lie, but she does swear!

(KERSTI *inclines her head again.*)

BRITA: Up with your head! Can't you look people in the eye?

KERSTI (*to the other girls*): Say something, girls!

(*Silence.*)

BRITA: It isn't easy to say what one hasn't seen. But . . . one knows what one knows all the same!

*

SHERIFF (*appears in the doorway*): I'm coming in—an old man may join the girls—though the boys have to stay out!

BRITA (*comes up to* KERSTI *and shakes her fist at her*): You are *not* going to have the crown!

KERSTI: Really!

(BRITA *goes out.*)

SHERIFF (*takes a chair and sits down directly in front of* KERSTI. *The* GIRLS *steal out, one by one. But* LILL-MATS *stays clinging to* KERSTI'*s skirt. The* SHERIFF *speaks in a friendly fashion, but when he wants to be nice he gets awkward and his words take on another meaning than the one he intended. Takes* KERSTI'*s hand and looks into her eyes*): Listen, Child! Should a bride

look so sad when she got the one she wanted? What's
wrong?

KERSTI (*coldly*): What's that?

SHERIFF (*strikes her cheek gently*): Is that the way to answer an
old friend who'll be your relative this time
tomorrow?—There are young girls who envy you and
would really have liked to be married ahead of you!

KERSTI: Maybe so.

SHERIFF: And the new life that awaits you, in the mill and the
kitchen. That won't be running about in the woods where
the wind blows and the birches sway, nor dancing in the
barn Saturday nights, but standing by the stove and sitting
by the cradle, and having food on the table when Mats
comes. And keeping up one's spirits when the dark days
come—for they always come just as rain follows sunlight.
Is it all that that frightens you, Child? The serious things in
life aren't so bad; they make life good and add dignity to it.
(KERSTI *sighs.*)

SHERIFF: What are you sighing for?—You do have something
on your mind a girl shouldn't have. Something
secret—let's see, Child, if I can guess.—(*Jokingly*)—a
policeman generally can get the truth out of anybody.
What are you worried about? Isn't Mats good to you?

KERSTI: Good heavens!

SHERIFF: Is it your in-laws who are high and mighty? What do
they concern you—
(LILL-MATS *climbs up into* KERSTI's *lap, puts his arms about
her neck; then he relaxes and falls asleep.*)

SHERIFF: Besides, look at that little rascal, he likes his
sister-in-law, and that's a good sign. Children can tell who
their friends are! Do you like children, Kersti?

KERSTI (*suspiciously*): Why do you ask that?

SHERIFF: For shame, such answers!—Isn't it wonderful to
have a little one like that—on one's lap and feel how he

clings to you? As if there weren't any deceit or doubt in your heart!—I think he's falling asleep, entrusting his helpless sleep to an outsider—who doesn't want to harm him!

KERSTI: Have you seen Mats?

SHERIFF: He was out with the boys getting the mill living room ready for the dance according to plans. *(Silence.)* It's been a long time since we had a crownbride here!

KERSTI: Really?

SHERIFF: Yes, indeed! New ways have come in—from the trips to the city and the military camps—[22]

KERSTI *(contemptuously)*: They used to blame the men who bought up the forest—

SHERIFF: Well, yes, but without them you would never have got the mill—

KERSTI: They blame, they blame—

SHERIFF: You're getting a good husband—

KERSTI: A good one—too good for me!

SHERIFF: Don't be bitter when I try to be friendly—

KERSTI: I was *not* bitter—that was the absolute truth I just said—

SHERIFF: We're having a hard time understanding each other—It looks as if we mayn't be friends—

KERSTI: Why not?

SHERIFF: When I mean well, you think the opposite, and vice versa! Yes—that's how it often is when something's wrong!

KERSTI: What is wrong?

SHERIFF *(gets up)*: I don't know.

KERSTI: I don't either, but you don't say that to a girl!

SHERIFF: Listen—a person can say something to someone with a clear conscience without offending—but, but, but—

KERSTI: Is this hearing over?

SHERIFF: It was *not* a hearing!

KERSTI: Sheriff—you can't talk with women.

SHERIFF (*sharply*): Kersti!

KERSTI: Well, what do you mean?

SHERIFF (*fixing her glance*): What do you mean?

KERSTI: What do you mean?

SHERIFF: That's what women I deal with ask when they want to know if I know something!

KERSTI: What should you know?

SHERIFF (*sighs*): Is that it?—Is that it?

(*Silence.*)

Well!—Then I suppose I'll go!—Then I'll go!

(*Goes out slowly through the door at the back with his finger on his mouth as if he were promising himself to say nothing.*)

(KERSTI *alone; kisses the sleeping* LILL-MATS *on the head.*)

MATS (*appears in the window to the right. It has begun to turn to dusk outside but there is still light*): Oh!

KERSTI: Mats! Come in!

MATS: No, I mayn't; I've promised!

KERSTI: Oh, come on!

MATS: No, no!—Is the little fellow sleeping?

KERSTI: Yes, that one! Sh-h, sh-h!

(*From the distance can be heard the trumpet call to regimental prayers.*)

Korum

KERSTI (*frightened*): Are they hunting again?
MATS: Oh no, they don't in the evening!
KERSTI: What then?
MATS: Surely a soldier's daughter knows that!
KERSTI: Well, tell me!
MATS: They're signaling for prayers in camp! Evening prayers, of course!
KERSTI: I suppose! Everything's so turned around and confused!
MATS: Come over to the window, Kersti!
KERSTI: I will—Just let me put the little one down first!
MATS: *That* little one?
KERSTI (*gets up carefully, walks on her toes carrying* LILL-MATS *to the bench by the fireplace, puts him down, and covers him*): Sh-h! sh-h! sh-h!
(*The singing of a hymn at the camp can be heard.*)
(KERSTI *falls to her knees by the bench, tries to pray but twists her hands in despair. Then she kisses the child, gets up, goes over to the window, where she stands motionless.*)
MATS: Children are fun, aren't they?
KERSTI: Yes!—Yes!
MATS: You were alone?
KERSTI: Yes, they left! Everything's unfriendly! Everything!
MATS: Tomorrow comes the wedding!
KERSTI: Yes!—Imagine!
MATS: Yes, imagine!—Tomorrow comes the wedding!
KERSTI: And then I'll be stuck in the mill!
MATS: With *me* in the mill!
KERSTI: Until death comes to part us!
MATS: That's far off!
(KERSTI *sighs.*)

[CURTAIN]

Scene 4

The wedding. The living room at the mill has been cleared. The doors at the back have been lifted off—one can see into a large storeroom arranged as a festive room with tables set for serving coffee, etc. The shutters to the large oblong opening to the upper left of the back entrance have been taken away so that a table with candles for the FIDDLERS *can be seen.*

To the right of the back entrance is the opening for the waterwheel; the loom, the bed, etc. have been removed.

On the floor below the place for the FIDDLERS *is a table with jugs, mugs, pipes, and playing cards, etc. for the* OLD MEN.

In the middle of the floor are benches and chairs over which clean white sheets, pillowcases, and hand towels are spread for drying.

Six HIRED GIRLS *are grinding coffee while one can hear from the distance the ringing of church bells and a wedding march played by violins. Then while they are gathering and putting together the sheets, etc., the* GIRLS *sing.*

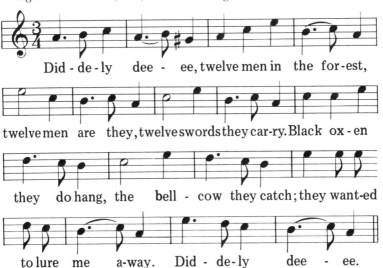

Did - de - ly   dee - ee, twelve men in the for-est,
twelve men are   they, twelve swords they car-ry. Black ox - en
they   do hang, the   bell - cow they catch; they want-ed
to lure me   a-way. Did - de-ly   dee - ee.

The wedding party approaches. The HIRED GIRLS *go out with their "washing" and then return to place benches and chairs on both sides of the room. Then the stage is empty, and it becomes silent outside until the* RIVER SPRITE *can be heard singing in the water wheel without being seen.*

RIVER SPRITE:
"I do hope, I do hope,
that my Redeemer still liveth."

The trapdoor on the floor opens and the MOCKER[23] *comes up out of a chaos of white veils in which one can see clearly the outline of a little child in a long christening dress, which flutters above the trapdoor. Then one hears the wedding march outside; the* RIVER SPRITE *becomes silent; the* MOCKER *disappears.*

The wedding party appears in the back room, first the FIDDLERS, *then the* BRIDESMAIDS, *and the* GROOM'S MEN; *then the* BRIDE *and the* BRIDEGROOM; *the* PASTOR, *the* PARENTS, *other* RELATIVES, GUESTS, *etc.*

The wedding party marches into the mill living room, silent and dejected. The BRIDE *is placed on a chair in the middle of the room back of the trapdoor so that she has to look at it. Now the people begin to circulate and move past the* BRIDE, *who is pale and looks down at the floor in front of her. One by one they go up to the* BRIDE, *say a few words to her and then go out into the back room.*

MATS (*to* KERSTI): Kersti, the worst is over! (*Goes.*)

BRITA (*comes up with the* BRIDESMAIDS *and says to* KERSTI): You have the crown; take good care of it! (*Leaves with the* BRIDESMAIDS.)

KERSTI'S MOTHER (*straightens the crown on* KERSTI'S *head*): Straighten up, Child, and raise your head! (*Goes.*)

SOLDIER (*to* KERSTI): God bless you! (*Goes.*)

VERGER (*to* KERSTI): And keep you! (*Goes.*)

MATS'S GRANDFATHER (*to* KERSTI): You are lovely as the dawn! (*Goes.*)

MATS'S MOTHER (*to* KERSTI): Welcome into the family! (*Goes.*)

MATS'S FATHER (*to* KERSTI): After this, my daughter—What's past doesn't exist! (*Goes.*)

SHERIFF (*to* KERSTI): How pale you are! Your blood has gone to your heart! What's so heavy?

KERSTI (*raises her head and looks angrily at the* SHERIFF): Nothing!

SHERIFF: Nothing *was* a lot! Nothing *is* nothing now!. . .

KERSTI: Go!

SHERIFF: When you ride, I'll walk ahead! Where you're going, I'm not following!—If you fall to your knees, I'll stand!—Who's throwing steel after you?[24] Not I!

KERSTI: Break your neck, you devil!

SHERIFF (*placing the flat of his hand on her throat*): Yours! (*Goes.*)

*

The rest of the relatives go by greeting her coldly. The FIDDLERS *have sat down at their table. The* OLD MEN *have sat down by the old men's table and are smoking. The* FIDDLERS *begin playing a polka.*)

(At the same time, the RIVER SPRITE's *violin can be heard from the waterwheel playing the following penetratingly. It is produced by two violins.)*

1:0

2:0

ad libitum

(When the dance music begins, cries from the back room can be heard): The crown off the bride! *(From the living room comes the answer)*: The crown off the bride!

    (KERSTI *becomes uneasy.)*

    (The PASTOR *approaches her.)*

FIDDLERS *(who now notice the* RIVER SPRITE's *playing, call out)*: Who's that playing?

ALL *(without looking at the wheel and without knowing from where the music is coming call out)*: Who's that playing?

    (The music continues; the RIVER SPRITE *becomes silent. Then the* PASTOR *takes the* BRIDE's *hand and promenades with her in a dignified fashion about the room. Just as he is about to put his arm about the* BRIDE's *waist to begin the dance, the* RIVER SPRITE *resumes his playing.)*

KERSTI *(drops the crown, which rolls down into the mill chute)*: Lord Jesus!

ALL *(in the mill living room rise and shout)*: The crown's in the rapids!

ALL *(in the back room)*: What's happening?

ALL (*in the living room*): The crown's in the rapids! (*The music abruptly stops. General excitement.*)

MATS (*in the doorway at the back*): Out and search for it!

ALL: Out and search!

PASTOR: Preserve us, God! in Heaven!

ALL: God in Heaven, preserve us!

SHERIFF: Out and search!

MATS: Out and search!

(ALL *go out at the back except* KERSTI, *who sits down on the chair; dusk has fallen; the wheel starts going; the* RIVER SPRITE *appears with his harp and sings his song.*

When the song begins, the trapdoor at KERSTI'S *feet opens, and the* MURDERED CHILD *rises as before.* KERSTI *looks at it first with horror; then she extends her arms and takes it into her arms. The* RIVER SPRITE *becomes silent and disappears. A* CHILD'S VOICE [*the* MOCKER'S] *can be heard from below the trapdoor.*)

CHILD'S VOICE: The river's cold, my mother's breast is warm! You gave me nothing in life; in death I'll take what's mine!

KERSTI (*who has at first sung softly to the* CHILD *now makes gestures of agony toward her bosom*): Help me! Save me!

CHILD'S VOICE: A life for a life! Now I drink yours!

KERSTI (*screams*): Save me, save me!

*

MIDWIFE (*enters, says fawningly*): There, there, now I'm here, I'm here! Calm yourself, little mother! (*Takes the* CHILD *from* KERSTI *and puts it into the opening.*) I can really take care of such little ones! I bring them into the world and into the ground!—So I did come to the wedding!

(BRITA *has appeared in the* FIDDLERS' *area and has seen that something was hidden in the opening.*)

MIDWIFE: Well, the River Sprite was invited, too. Did he come?

KERSTI: What would you take for leaving?

MIDWIFE: What you no longer have!

KERSTI: You mean the crown—

MIDWIFE: Not particularly!—Sh-h, someone's walking up there!—Then I'll hide in the stove for the time being!—You see, I did come all the same! (*Goes into the fireplace-stove and shuts the ventilators after her.*)

BRITA (*comes in; up to* KERSTI): Now it's either you or I!

KERSTI: You!

BRITA: You're to get something!

KERSTI: Give it to me!

BRITA: You'll get a bracelet, but not from me! (*Silence.*) A bracelet of iron! (*Stands on the trapdoor.*) Now I'm treading on your head, now I'm standing on your heart, now I'm stamping your secret out of the earth, or the water, or the fire. (*Silence.*) Now I'll get your hair, now I'll get my watchchain, which isn't one really. Where's the midwife, where's the guest of honor at this virginal wedding? You stole the crown, and the River Sprite stole it! You stole the mill, but it will revert! Shechem's Dina was ruined, not spoiled! The little one sleeps, not in the forest, but in the stream! You have shamed my brother, you have shamed my people, you have shamed my name! You shall die!

KERSTI (*submissively*): I *am* dead; I have died day after day!—Are you satisfied?

BRITA: You shall die still more days to come! You shall die for perjury, for lying, for killing, for theft, for insult, for deceit! You shall die six times! and the seventh will be only for the sake of appearance!—You shall not rest in consecrated earth, you shall not get a black coffin with silver stars, nor spruce branches and ringing of bells.—[25]

KERSTI: I imagine not!

BRITA: So—do you hear the steps? Count them: one, two,

three, four, five, six . . . (*Etc. according to the* SHERIFF's
steps.)

    (*The* SHERIFF *enters from in back.*)

    (BRITA *goes up to him and whispers something.*)

SHERIFF (*goes up to the trapdoor*): It is here!

BRITA: Surely not the crown!

SHERIFF: That or something else! (*Opens the trapdoor.*) It isn't
the crown! Poor Kersti!—Have you put it here?

KERSTI: No!

SHERIFF: No?—Tell the truth!

KERSTI: I did not put it there!

BRITA (*slaps her on the mouth*): The truth!

KERSTI: I did not put it there!

BRITA (*puts her hand into the* SHERIFF's *pockets and takes out
handcuffs*): On with the bracelets!

SHERIFF (*to* BRITA): Born to be a hangman's
woman—(*Weeps, his hands to his eyes.*)

*

PASTOR (*enters from the back*): Have you found it?

SHERIFF: Not that! But—

PASTOR: Don't say any more! I know—(*Weeps, his hands
to his eyes.*)

*

SOLDIER (*enters from the back*): Have you found the crown?

SHERIFF: Not that! But—

SOLDIER: Sh-h, I know—(*Weeps, his hands to his eyes.*)

*

KERSTI'S MOTHER (*enters from the back*): Have you found the
crown?

SHERIFF: Oh, no!

MOTHER (*looks at* KERSTI *who extends her hands toward the
handcuffs which* BRITA *is extending toward her, screams. Then
she takes up a pair of scissors and cuts off* KERSTI's *hair, which*

she throws to BRITA, *who grabs it and smells it as if it were fragrant. The* MOTHER *tears off the bridal veil and the bridal ornaments and throws a towel over* KERSTI'*s head.*)

MATS (*enters from in back; stops in front of* KERSTI *and looks at her with amazement*): Who is *this?*

BRITA: Take a close look!

MATS (*looks at her more closely:*) She looks like someone!

BRITA: Take a close look!

MATS: I don't know her!

BRITA: Would that you had never known her!

MATS: See, her eyes are gone! But her mouth, her lovely mouth—and the little chin—No, it isn't she! (*Turns away and sees the open trapdoor*). What's there? You're standing as if around a grave!

BRITA: It is a grave!

MATS: What's in it?

BRITA: Everything! Everything that was worthwhile in your life!

MATS: Then it's the little one!—Who has done this to me?

BRITA: She, she and she!

MATS: That's a lie!

  (ALL *who have been outside have come in and gathered in the background.*)

BRITA: It is true!

MATS: Liar!

SOLDIER (*to* BRITA): Liar out of a family of liars!

MATS'S RELATIVES (*gather to the left of* KERSTI): Family of liars, of thieves! You! You!

KERSTI'S RELATIVES (*gather to the right*): You! You!

PASTOR: Peace! Peace! In the name of the Lord!

ALL: Peace!

SHERIFF: No one's to judge in advance!

ALL: Let's hear!

SHERIFF: Who's the plaintiff?

BRITA: I, Brita Lisa Larsson.
ALL: Brita Lisa Larsson's the plaintiff. Against whom?
BRITA: Against Kersti Margreta Hansdotter!
ALL: Against Kersti Margreta Hansdotter!—What's the charge?
BRITA: If the bride's spoiled, she doesn't get the crown!
KERSTI'S RELATIVES: Proof, proof!
BRITA: Two witnesses are enough!
MATS'S RELATIVES: Two witnesses are enough!
KERSTI'S RELATIVES: We challenge them!
SHERIFF: You have to have grounds!
BRITA: An unmarried woman gives birth in secret; if the child dies, the mother loses her life!
MATS'S RELATIVES: Loses her life!
KERSTI'S RELATIVES:(*move threateningly toward* MATS'S RELATIVES): Shame!
MATS'S RELATIVES: Shame!
KERSTI'S RELATIVES: A bad and bitter man doesn't know he's full of flaws! Mats is to blame!
MATS'S RELATIVES: Mats is not to blame!
KERSTI'S RELATIVES: Mats is to blame for he did it!
MATS'S RELATIVES (*their hands lifted*): Did he? Ask Kersti!
KERSTI'S RELATIVES: Let's ask her!
SHERIFF (*to* KERSTI): Did you kill the child?
KERSTI: Yes!
MATS'S RELATIVES: Hear that!
      (KERSTI'S RELATIVES *sigh with dismay.*)
MATS'S RELATIVES: Hear that!

*

MATS (*who has been standing deep in thought by the fireplace with his back to everything, now throws the things indicating he is the bridegroom on the floor; stands still for a moment; then he rushes as if beside himself up on the old men's table and out through the fiddlers' area*): "How wonderful it was, how ugly it is now!" Kersti dear, the little one's asleep in the forest!

PASTOR (*his head in his hands weeps; then he says, beside the open trapdoor*):
"Lord Jesus,
grant the dead peace.
Comfort those
who are living!"
(ALL *pray silently as people recite the Lord's Prayer in church or at the graveside.*)

PASTOR: The Lord bless you and keep you!

ALL (*weeping*): Amen! (*They go out, silent and mournful.*)

*

(*When* KERSTI *alone remains, the* SHERIFF *closes and locks the doors at the back, then the one in the fiddlers' area; then there is a loud thundering noise from the fireplace-stove.* KERSTI *jumps up, terrified.*)

RIVER SPRITE (*appears in the millwheel and sings as he plays his violin*):
"I do hope, I do hope,
that my Redeemer still liveth!"
(*Several times.*)

(KERSTI *on her knees with her handcuffed hands raised upwards.*)

The CHILD IN WHITE *appears from behind the fireplace; has a basket with spruce twigs and flowers. The* RIVER SPRITE *becomes silent and disappears. The* CHILD *strews spruce twigs before him so that a path is formed to the trapdoor. When he comes up to this he strews flowers down into the opening. The harmonica can be heard; its music resembles that of church bells.*

Then he goes back of KERSTI, *who does not see him, and places his hands gently over her head and looks upward as if he were praying.*

KERSTI's *face, which had expressed despair, now looks calm and happy.*

[CURTAIN]

SCENE 5

To the right an open porch of a country church. It is brightly whitewashed; the roof of black timbers. KERSTI *is lying on the penitent's stool in prison garb with a hood over her head. The background: a lake and Dalarna landscape; to the front a boat landing. To the right at the back a headland juts down into the lake, and on this can be seen the pillory consisting of a platform and a block.*

At the entrance to the porch two armed SOLDIERS *are standing at ease.*

Organ preludes can be heard from the church—

Two large church boats come to the landing, one from the left, the other from the right. The boats glide in, the rowers holding their oars lifted. It looks as if they were arguing about the order of boat landing.

MATS'S RELATIVES *are in the left boat;* KERSTI's, *in the right boat.*

MATS'S RELATIVES: Out of the way, Killers!

KERSTI'S RELATIVES: Out of the way, Millers!

MATS'S RELATIVES (*raise their oars threateningly*): Out of the way!

KERSTI'S RELATIVES (*make threatening gestures with their oars*): Out of the way!

MATS'S RELATIVES: Can you put up eight pair?

KERSTI'S RELATIVES: Sixteen if need be!—Hit 'em!

MATS'S RELATIVES: Hit! Hit! Hit!

(*Both groups fence with their oars.*)

PASTOR (*bareheaded in the front of the boat to the left*):
Peace!—Peace in the name of the Lord!

KERSTI'S RELATIVES: Peace!

MATS'S RELATIVES: No!

PASTOR: Peace!

MATS'S RELATIVES: No!

*

VERGER (*comes out from the church porch, pulls the rope and rings
the bells*). (*The oars are lowered, the boats glide into the landing
side by side. Out of the left boat comes first the* PASTOR, *then*
MATS *carrying a small white coffin trimmed with lace. Then all
of* MATS'S RELATIVES *and* FRIENDS.)

Out of the boat to the right: first the SOLDIER, then KERSTI'S
MOTHER and then all KERSTI'S RELATIVES and FRIENDS. Both
parties adjust their clothes and observe each other with angry
looks.

MATS comes forward with the coffin, followed by the PASTOR.

MATS (*stops in front of* KERSTI; *he looks beside himself*): The little
one's here! He's as light as an evil woman's mind! Now he
sleeps—soon you'll sleep!

KERSTI (*lifts her head so that the hood drops down*): O!

MATS: Say O! That's the end; but A's the beginning! Between
A and O lie many letters, but O's the last one![26] Say O now
for the very last time—so that the little one hears it! He's
to tell the Lord and Savior about it so you'll receive
forgiveness!—Yes!—Kiss the casket then, down by the
small feet, the tiny, tiny feet, which never had time to
tramp this sinful earth!

(KERSTI *kisses the coffin.*)

MATS: There!—Now we're going in to play and sing and ring
the bells for the little one—but we won't get the pastor to

read for him—that's your fault!—but I'll read myself when
we come to the grave! We will put him in the earth as a
seed that's to lie there growing into a heart flower with
wings on it so that he can fly to God afterwards—on a puff
of wind in the midsummer sun!
PASTOR (*takes* MATS *by the arm*): That will do, Mats! Come
along!
MATS: I'm coming!
(*They go into the church, the rest follow slowly.*)
SOLDIER (*stops for a moment in front of* KERSTI, *shakes his head
sorrowfully and tries to get out a few words*): Yes!—Yes! (*Goes
into the church.*)
KERSTI'S MOTHER (*dryly with an attempt to be sympathetic*): So
we meet again!—Have you had a hard time in prison?
(KERSTI *shakes her head.*)
MOTHER: Do you want anything? To eat or drink?—You may
now! Did you get tobacco in prison?
(KERSTI *shakes her head.*)
MOTHER: Keep your head up, Kersti, so the millfolk can't
laugh at us!—And don't cry so much! Your father's a
soldier, and he can't stand that! (*Hands her a psalmbook.*)
Take this book—and read, where the marker is. Look at
the marker—I got it from someone—who will think of
you to the very last! And that helps against trembling!—I
won't go with you any farther, Kersti, for I can't! I can't,
because I'm old—
KERSTI: It doesn't matter, Mother! I've found my comforter,
for I know my Redeemer lives!
MOTHER: Then it's all right, Child! That was all I wanted to
know!—And you don't insist I should go with—
KERSTI: No, Mother; spare yourself. Haven't I made it hard
enough for you?
MOTHER: Then I'll count on the millfolk's not getting
anything to comment on! I'll count on it so I can say: Kersti

wanted it that way. Kersti wanted it like that, and her last request's like unwritten law!—Yes, it is! (*Goes into the church.*)

*

BRITA (*pointing toward the pillory*): You were born a queen, you got the crown, there you have your throne, Heaven is above, Hell below!—Now you'd like to milk cows; now you'd like to pick up sticks for the fire, scrub the kettle, lull the smallest one to sleep, polish shoes, yes now, when you've disgraced my family, your family, our parish, our district, our province, so that the whole country's talking about what you did!

(KERSTI *bows her head over the psalmbook.*)

BRITA: My brother has to carry your bastard to the grave—my brother, you bitch! But I'll follow you to the stocks; when you'll be whipped, I'll go with you as a bridesmaid to your scarlet bridal stool! "It's a corpse, but isn't dead; it's a child, but isn't born; there's a bride, but not a wedding!"

*

LILL-MATS: Shut up, Brita! Kersti's nice!

BRITA: Huh!

LILL-MATS: Yes, she is! But she shouldn't wear that ugly coat, for you should, Brita!—Kersti! Why are you lying here? Is there communion today? And why did you leave the wedding? Who was in the white box? Is it a fairytale? Did you know I've lost my doll that you gave me?—Kersti! Why are you sad? (*Clings to her;* KERSTI *hugs him and kisses his feet.*)

KERSTI: Lill-Mats, Lill-Mats!

BRITA (*to the* SOLDIERS): Is that permitted?

(*The* SOLDIERS *straighten up but do not answer.*)

BRITA (*takes* LILL-MATS *from* KERSTI): Come on!

KERSTI (*to* LILL-MATS): Go with your sister, Lill-Mats! And stay away from me! (*Reads softly in the psalmbook.*)

BRITA (*to* KERSTI): Shall I tell him?

KERSTI: For Heaven's sake, don't tell the child!

BRITA: I shan't tell for the child's sake!

KERSTI: Thank you, Brita! Thank you for the child's sake!

> (BRITA *goes* into the church with LILL-MATS. *All the rest have gone in.*)   *

> (*At the back right the* HANGMAN *comes in with a black box under his arm.*)

KERSTI (*becomes aware of him without his looking at her*): Christ Jesus, Savior of the world, help me! In the name of Your suffering and death!   *

MIDWIFE (*enters from the left and goes up to the* HANGMAN): Listen, listen! May I stand alongside—if you do it—? I need a little red blood for a sick person, a person who has the falling sickness!

> (*The* HANGMAN *goes out to the left without answering.*)

MIDWIFE: So-o! He's one of those you can't talk to! (*Up to* KERSTI.) There you are, dear—

KERSTI (*makes a gesture of rejection*): Get thee gone!

MIDWIFE (*back of a pillar, not seen by the* SOLDIERS): Wait a minute, wait a minute! Listen, little innocent!—What others can't do, I can!—The clock'll strike soon, and Satan's waiting!—

KERSTI: In the name of Jesus, get thee gone!

MIDWIFE: Listen!—I can do what others can't. I can help you get free!

KERSTI: I have found my helper! Lord Jesus!

MIDWIFE: But I can deafen the judge—

KERSTI: The One who judges the living and the dead, He who is the life and the resurrection has condemned me to earthly death and—eternal life.

MIDWIFE: Look at the soldiers who are sleeping; take my cape and run!

KERSTI: The soldiers are sleeping?

MIDWIFE: With eyes closed!—Run, run, run!

(KERSTI *gets up, looks at the* SOLDIERS, *who have closed their eyes.*)

MIDWIFE: Run, run, run!

KERSTI (*lies down again*): No! I'd rather fall into the hands of the living God! Get thee gone!

(*She lifts the psalmbook with the golden cross on its cover*).

MIDWIFE (*shrinks back*): Shall we meet one Thursday night at the crossroads?

KERSTI: On the way of the cross I'll meet my Redeemer, but not with you! Get thee gone!

MIDWIFE (*shrinks back*): There's a boat by the shore, and there's a horse and a cart on shore—Mats is there, too, but the sheriff isn't there—Run, run, run!

KERSTI (*struggling with herself*): God, lead us not into temptation but deliver us from evil!

MIDWIFE (*hisses*): Horse and cart!

(KERSTI *grasps the church bell's rope and tolls it three times; at the third stroke, the* MIDWIFE *flees, hissing.*)

*

(*The* CHILD IN WHITE *comes from in back of a pillar. He is dressed in a Rättvik's girls' folk costume,*[27] *but everything is white, even his shoes.*)

KERSTI (*as if blinded*): Who are you, Child, who comes when the evil one goes?

(*The* CHILD *puts his finger to his mouth.*)

KERSTI: White as snow, white as flax!—Why are you white?

CHILD (*softly*): Your faith has saved you! Faith has borne hope! (*Approaches* KERSTI).

KERSTI: Dear, don't step on the ant!

CHILD (*bends down and picks up something on a leaf*): But the greatest is love, love for everything living, big and small—Now the ant may go to the forest to tell the king of ants,[28] and his folk will come to gnaw your ropes and you're free!

KERSTI: Oh no! Don't say that!

CHILD: Don't doubt! but believe! believe! Kersti!—Believe!

KERSTI: How can I?

CHILD: Believe! (*Goes out, back of the pillar*).

(*It darkens.*)

RIVER SPRITE (*can be seen on the lake with his harp. Sings*):
"I do hope, I do hope,
   that your Redeemer still liveth!"

KERSTI: He sings about the Redeemer for me! He gives me hope! but I gave him nothing!

(*The* RIVER SPRITE *sinks into the depths.*)

*

SHERIFF (*enters from the right, reading a document; comes up to* KERSTI *stopping now and then, now looking down at the ground, now at the document*): Kersti!

(KERSTI *looks up; then bows her head immediately.*)

SHERIFF (*slowly, with pauses*): Look at the Sheriff!—You only fear him!—Does everyone?—Think of this, when someone sends for me because he needs help. Isn't he welcome then? Oh yes!—Kersti, have you ever seen so many ants?

(KERSTI *raises her head and becomes attentive.*)

SHERIFF: Look, how they run in bunches and in rows!—Just look!—Do you know what that means?—Something good is going to happen!—You never believe any good about me. You didn't believe me *that* time either—so you were exposed!—Look at the ants! Just look at them! Now they're coming on you, Kersti!—Aren't you afraid of them?

KERSTI: I have been, but I'm not!

SHERIFF: Big forest ants, and I think the king himself is along. What can the king do that other officials can't? Do you know?—The rest can judge; everyone can judge, severely or not severely! But only one can grant a pardon! That one is the king!—Shall we ask the king of ants if he grants you a pardon? (*He puts his hand to his ear as if he wanted to listen.*) Will you, king of the ants, grant a pardon, that's to say from the worst?—Did you hear what he answered?—I thought he said yes!—But I may have misheard—And I don't rely on hearsay; I'm a sheriff and want it in black and white,—We'll ask the king of ants to write, he has so many pens in the forest, small steel pens sharp as needles; and he has the ink himself, and that stings! If we only had a piece of paper! (*Pretends to search in his pocket and takes out the document he has just been reading.*) Well, well!—The king has written this with his own hand! There it says C,A,R,L, that's Carl![29] (*Raises his cap.*) You haven't seen such large letters since you went to school, Kersti. And the red seal, which is as fragrant as resin in the forest when it's warm!—And then the blue and yellow silk cord—and the lion and the crowns—it is royal—Read it yourself, Kersti, and I'll give the orders to the soldiers!

(KERSTI *accepts the document.*)

(*The* SHERIFF *speaks softly to the* SOLDIERS *who then leave.*)

(KERSTI *has read the pardon and returns it to the* SHERIFF *calmly and with dignity.*)

SHERIFF: Are you glad, Kersti?

KERSTI: I'm thankful my relatives and yours have got out of the *greatest* shame. I'm not glad, for a life in chains is less than eternal life.

SHERIFF: Take it as a time of preparation!

KERSTI: I will!

SHERIFF: Are you still afraid of me?

KERSTI: I'm not afraid of anything any more since I have faced death!

SHERIFF: Then come with me!

KERSTI: Untie the ropes then!
(*The* SHERIFF *does. The organ prelude can be heard.* KERSTI *raises her hands toward the sky.*)

[CURTAIN]

SCENE 6

The background is a large, ice-covered lake with its shores in the distance. The ice is covered with snow. The floor of the stage represents the ice. On this can be seen the winter road marked with pine branches. A large oblong hole in the ice for seine fishing at stage center toward the back. At the edge of this rest ducks (divers who utter melodious cries occasionally). Around the hole are small fishpoles for fishing on ice. At the very back of the stage "the Castle" (the Prison), an ugly old building with towers and pinnacles. It is dawning.

(*A* FISHERMAN *enters from the right, in a fur coat, with sled and icepick; the ducks dive down into the hole. The* FISHERMAN *begins to take up his lines.*)

MIDWIFE (*enters from the left*): Should you be fishing on Easter morning?

FISHERMAN: I'm not fishing, I'm just checking!

MIDWIFE: You who are so wise tell this old woman who has lost her way where she is.

FISHERMAN: If you'll lend me fire, I will.

MIDWIFE: Give me flint and steel then!

FISHERMAN (*hands her two pieces of ice*): Take these!

MIDWIFE: Ice? Well, water's fire, and fire's water! (*Strikes the two pieces of ice against each other after she has torn tinder from her cape; hands the lighted tinder to the* FISHERMAN *who lights his pipe with it.*)

FISHERMAN: So you are one of those! Then I know where I'm at!

MIDWIFE: But where am I?

FISHERMAN: You're in the middle of Krummedikke's Lake,[30] and there's their castle. Long ago Krummedikke was a king who, like Herod, had all the boy children killed because he was afraid he'd lose his crown. But nowadays all the girls who haven't been careful about their crowns are in that castle.

MIDWIFE: What are they doing there?

FISHERMAN: Spinning flax!

MIDWIFE: It's a house of correction?

FISHERMAN: That's what it is!

MIDWIFE: What about the lake?

FISHERMAN: Well, that *is* something! Where the lake is used to be land, and there was a church on the land. There was contention in that church—about pews; the Millfolk, who were considered better people, wanted to sit closest to the altar, but the Killers were stronger. They went at it one Easter day in the center aisle, and blood flowed. The church was desecrated and could never be scrubbed clean. So it was closed and deserted; and it sank into the earth and fifteen ells of water rose over the rooster on the tower spire. And the water has washed and washed away at it many hundred years, but as long as the Millfolk and the Killers fight each other, the House of God can never be cleansed.

MIDWIFE: Why are they called Killers?

FISHERMAN: Because they're descendants of the child murderer Krummedikke!

MIDWIFE: They're still contending?

FISHERMAN: Contending still and murdering still!—You remember—Kersti, the soldier's daughter?

MIDWIFE: Yes, indeed!

FISHERMAN: She's in the castle, but today she's to do her annual penance in church!

MIDWIFE: Really!

FISHERMAN: The Killers are going to fetch her, and the millfolk are coming to look on!

MIDWIFE: Did you hear—the ice is cracking?

FISHERMAN: Yes, indeed!

MIDWIFE: Will it thaw?

FISHERMAN: Probably!

MIDWIFE: Then the ice will loosen from the shore?

FISHERMAN: Most likely!—But if the water rises, it'll run out over the waterfall down there!

MIDWIFE: Is it far to the waterfall?

FISHERMAN: No!—You can hear the River Sprite from here.—Today he's up early, because he's expecting something!

MIDWIFE: What can he expect?

FISHERMAN: You know what he's expecting!—

MIDWIFE: I don't know! Tell me!

FISHERMAN: This is what's said! Every Easter morning, when the Savior rises from the grave, the Krummedikke Church rises from the lake! And the one who gets to see it has peace all year!

(*The* MIDWIFE *gallops out to the right, hissing.*)

FISHERMAN: That was an evil one!—(*He pulls up a fish and frees it from the hook. Laughs. The fish jumps into the water. The* FISHERMAN *tries to catch it with his handnet. A whole row of fish heads stick up out of the hole.*) Dumb, but not deaf! "Who calls more loudly than the crane? Who is whiter than the swan?"

CHILD IN WHITE (*dressed in white Rättvik girls' folk costume comes in on skis carrying a lighted torch*): The thunder of heaven cries higher than the crane! The one who never does evil is whiter than the swan! (*The fish disappear.*)

FISHERMAN: Who solved my riddle?

CHILD: Who loosened the prisoner's chains? Who loosened the fish's tongue?

FISHERMAN: No one!

CHILD: No one born of man but someone born of the creative God.—The one who built the bridge of glass can break it!—Take care! (*Goes out at right.*)

(*The* FISHERMAN *gathers his fishing equipment.*)

*

The MILLFOLK, MATS'S *relatives, enter from the left on skis carrying staffs;* MATS *is carrying a torch.*

MATS: Where's the winter road?

FISHERMAN: Did you see the fish's road in the water?

MATS: But the horse's in the snow!

FISHERMAN: On your way to court or to church?

MILLFOLK: Church!

FISHERMAN: For the one who has gone astray all roads lead to the waterfall! (*The ice cracks loudly.*) The roof's breaking up!

MILLFOLK: Where's the road to church?

FISHERMAN: Everywhere!

MILLFOLK: Where's the church?

FISHERMAN: You're standing on it, you're walking on it; it'll soon be here.

MILLFOLK: Is this Krummedikke's lake?

FISHERMAN: It's Krummedikke's lake and Krummedikke's castle and Krummedikke's church; soon there'll be water on the ice!

MILLFOLK: The Lord preserve us! (*Exit to right.*)

*

KILLERS: (KERSTI's *relatives come in from the left on skis with staffs. The* SOLDIER *is carrying a torch*): Where's the church road?

FISHERMAN: This leads to the waterfall! Turn back!

KILLERS: Piles of ice and open water! The ice has broken free of the shore.

FISHERMAN: Go east! The sun's still up!

KILLERS: East! (*Exit to the right.*)

*

(*The* MILLFOLK *reenter from the right.*)

FISHERMAN: Turn back! The ice has broken free of the shore to the west!

MILLFOLK: And to the east!—Let's go north!

FISHERMAN: The river's to the north!

MILLFOLK: We'll go south!

FISHERMAN: The rapids are there!

MILLFOLK (*rest on their staffs, discouraged*): God be gracious unto us!

*

MATS: The Killers led us astray!

BRITA: The Killers always did!

FATHER: And first place in church!

GRANDFATHER: Doesn't matter! But the day I burned the papers I do not bless!

MOTHER: When will we get peace?

GRANDMOTHER: "The noble and the gentle live most happily and seldom suffer sorrow."[31]

MILLFOLK (*raise their staffs*): The Killers!

*

KILLERS (*enter from right again with lifted staffs*): Millfolk! Stand! You have led us astray!

MILLFOLK: Liars!

KILLERS: Liars yourselves!

MILLFOLK: Wordtwisters!

KILLERS: Wordtwisters yourselves!

(*The ice cracks loudly.*)

FISHERMAN: Peace in the name of Christ! The water's rising!

ALL (*scream out*): The water's rising!

MATS'S GRANDFATHER: The ice is sinking! Stay where you are!

MATS'S GRANDMOTHER: For we must die! And then the judgment!

(*The* MILLFOLK *embrace each other; the women take the children up into their arms; the* KILLERS *do the same sorts of things among themselves.*) *

MATS'S MOTHER (*to* MATS): Because of your foolish love we must die!

KERSTI'S MOTHER: "Let no one blame another's love; beauty often captures the wise man, but not the fool."[32]

SOLDIER: "For this fault no one shall blame him. Mighty love makes the wise sons of men fools."[33]

MATS (*extends his hand to the* SOLDIER): Thank you for those words! I once called you father!

SOLDIER: Death makes us all equal—

MATS' FATHER: You have said what I meant to say. Your hand!

SOLDIER (*extends his hand with some hesitation*): Here it is!—We are Christians, and this is the great day of reconciliation! May the sun not go up over our wrath!

KILLERS: Reconciliation!

MILLFOLK: Reconciliation!

(*The two families approach each other with extended hands; but now the ice cracks loudly and parts so open water separates the two groups.*)

MATS'S GRANDFATHER: Parted in life, parted in death!

MATS'S GRANDMOTHER: The bridge broke under the burden of sin!

MATS'S MOTHER: Where is Kersti?

MILLFOLK: Where is Kersti?

KILLERS: Where is Kersti?

SOLDIER: "And lo, it was good that one died for the people!"

MATS'S GRANDFATHER: "Then they said to him: What shall we do with you so that the sea may become still for us?"

KERSTI'S MOTHER: "Take and cast me into the sea, for I know that this tempest has come upon you because of me."[34]

GRANDMOTHER: Is it settled?

ALL: It is settled!

KERSTI'S MOTHER: Lo, here is fire and wood. Where is the sacrificial lamb?[35]

KILLERS: Where is Kersti?

MILLFOLK: Where is Kersti?

*

(*The* PASTOR *enters accompanied by the* VERGER).

PASTOR (*to the* SOLDIER): "The Lord said: Lay not thine hand upon the child . . . for now I know that thou fearest God! and have not withheld thine only child for my sake!"[36]

ALL (*to the* PASTOR): Save us!

PASTOR: "There is but one God, the Savior!"—Let us pray!

(ALL *kneel.*)

PASTOR: Out of the depths I call unto Thee, O Lord!

ALL: Lord, hear my voice!

PASTOR: Lord, have mercy!

ALL: Christ, have mercy!

PASTOR: Lord, have mercy!

ALL: Christ, have mercy!

*

(*The* SHERIFF *enters from the back with a torch; accompanied by four* SOLDIERS *carrying* KERSTI'S *corpse.* ALL *rise.*)

PASTOR: Whom do you bring?

SHERIFF: We bring the crownbride; we bring Kersti.

PASTOR: Is she alive?

SHERIFF: She's dead! The water took her!

PASTOR: May the Lord take her soul!

SOLDIERS: Oh God, be merciful to our sacrifice as You sacrificed Yourself for us!

PASTOR: "For God so loved the world that He gave His only begotten son!"

BRITA: The water's sinking!

ALL: The water's sinking.

(*The gap in the ice closes.* MATS *and* BRITA *go over to the* KILLERS, *break up pine and spruce branches and lay them on* KERSTI.)

PASTOR: Do we have peace, now?

ALL: Peace! and reconciliation!

PASTOR (*beside* KERSTI'*s body*):
    "Lord Jesus!
    Grant the dead peace,
    Comfort those
    Who are living!"

(*Now the church rises out of the lake at the back; first the golden rooster, then the cross and the globe, afterwards the tower and the white Romanesque church with its black shake roof.*)

RIVER SPRITE (*sings in the distance, but now in subdued D-minor*):
    "I do hope, I do hope,
    that my Redeemer still liveth!"

PASTOR: Let us thank and praise the Lord!

ALL: The Lord be thanked and praised!

(MATS *and* BRITA *kneel beside* KERSTI'*s body.*)

ALL (*kneel, singing these verses from Number 6 in the Old Psalmbook*):
    O God, we praise Thee! O, Lord, we thank Thee!
    The whole world adores Thee, eternal Father.
    All angels, heavens and all powers praise Thee
    Cherubim and Seraphim sing without end
    Holy, holy, holy Lord the God almighty!

[CURTAIN]

Notes on 'The Crownbride'

1. A *fäbod*, here translated "upland farm," is a pasture area at some distance from the home farm or village and is used for summer grazing. Supplied with huts and sheds, the *fäbod* has from time immemorial been the summer home for women and men looking after cattle, churning butter, and making cheese.

2. The lure is a long curved trumpet for communicating with other herders and for calling cattle. The lure is generally made of pinewood covered by birch bark.

3. Tattleberries (*skvallerbär*) are any berries that leave a stain about the lips of the person who eats them. For example, blackberries and blueberries.

4. Part of cheesemaking.

5. Rural Swedes, not least those in Dalarna, have preserved many of the wedding practices from both pre-Christian and medieval days such as the bridal crown (symbol of virginity), the wedding procession and ritual, and post-wedding festivities.

6. Swedish folklore includes tales of supposedly supernatural hunts based on unusual noises during periods of quiet as well as during storms. Several writers have made effective use of such superstitions and tales, most notably perhaps Selma Lagerlöf in *Jerusalem* and, of course, Strindberg in this play.

7. The feud between the Montagues and the Capulets in *Romeo and Juliet* is an obvious parallel of this ancient motif.

8. The River Sprite (*Näcken* or *Strömkarlen*), according to Swedish folklore, is a mysterious being or lost soul who lives in streams or lakes, plays the violin beautifully, entices people into the water, takes those who drown, and, as Strindberg says, has a particularly hard time gaining salvation.

9. The patriarchal family scene is one that many Swedes elsewhere would have understood as typical of Dalarna, then and even now, a province in which old beliefs and customs have been preserved. Note the "Icelandic" (that is, laconic and pithy) speech, the women smoking pipes, the creation of objects from hair to sell on trips throughout the country, the respect for the elderly, the importance of family, and the nature of the family council.

10. The stanza is quoted from Hymn (*Psalm*) 278 in the 1695 Swedish hymnal (*Svenska psalmboken*).

11. Job 8:3.

12. Ecclesiastes 3:8.

13. Kersti's father was an "indelt soldat," that is, a soldier who in return for a locally supplied cottage, a small area of land to cultivate, and small buildings for animals served as a soldier ready to take part annually in training sessions and to serve fulltime in the army when needed. The system was changed in 1902 and disappeared completely in the 1940s.

14. The Dalesmen have had the reputation of being courageous but not foolhardy, always self-reliant but never obsequious, reticent but not unfeeling, proud but not vain.

15. Strindberg has obviously exploited the rich folklore of Dalarna, which includes colorful superstitions.

16. Quoted from the medieval Icelandic *Song of the Sun* (*Sólarljóð*, Swedish *Solsången*).

17. *Skratten* = the Laugher, the Mocker. *Mylingen* here is the murdered child. The fisherman says the killers (*mylingar*) are so called because of their slaying of a child. An older form of *myling* is *myrding*, based on *mörda* (to murder).

18. In Strindberg's account of Swedish weddings in the sixteenth century, he says (*Samlade skrifter*, VII, 431): "Maidens' evenings (*mökvällar*), proper parties the evening before the wedding, were to be celebrated." The term here translated Virgin's Eve, obviously applies to a ceremony of purification plus a highly subdued parallel to, say, the American bachelor party.

19. The practice of having a picture of the royal family conspicuously hung on the wall helps determine the time of the action—roughly the early part of the second half of the nineteenth

century. Charles (Carl) XV (1859–72) was Strindberg's benefactor in 1872 when he granted the young playwright a stipend.

20. See Note 13. Summer maneuvers are being held nearby as the music in the military church service and the reference to the reasons for the lack of crownbrides suggest. Kersti's father is on leave because of the wedding.

21. By all means read the thirty-fourth chapter of Genesis!

22. *Dalkullor* (girls in Dalarna) traveled about Sweden in Kersti's day selling goods such as the hair chain Brita is making. The danger of corruption in the cities is linked with similar dangers from soldiers quartered nearby and from lumberjacks working in the forests.

23. See Note 17.

24. According to superstition, steel could be used as a detector of and protection against evil.

25. Murderers, suicides, and unbaptized children could not be buried in cemeteries but in "unhallowed" ground outside the churchyard. Strindberg says (in *Samlade skrifter,* VII, 264): "The north side of the churchyard was considered profane and on that were buried only suicides and unbaptized children."

26. Refers to "alpha and omega" (the beginning and the end of the Greek alphabet).

27. Swedish folk costumes have varied not only from province to province but from parish to parish. The Rättvik costume for girls has a dark blue skirt, a green-red-and-white striped apron, a white blouse, and a red and green cap. The costume here required includes a blouse, a skirt, an apron, and a cap—all in white.

28. The role of the king of ants and his folk in assisting human beings in need is a striking part of the folktales about the insects.

29. Charles XV (Carl). See n. 19 above.

30. The tall folktale is used for various purposes: to emphasize the folk's faith in miracles, their willingness to suspend disbelief and extend their imaginations, and their firm faith in morality.

31. See, for example, Stanza 6 of "Hávamál" ("The Speech or Song of the High One") in *The Poetic Edda.*

32. Ibid., Stanza 93.

33. Ibid., Stanza 94.

34. Jonah 1:11, 12.

35. See, for example, Genesis 22:7 (". . . where *is* the lamb for a burnt offering?").

36. Genesis 22:12.

Introduction to 'Swanwhite'

IN HIS *Open Letters to the Intimate Theater*, Strindberg explained that his major sources of inspiration for *Swanwhite*, written in 1901, were Maeterlinck's marionette plays, medieval folktales, and early Swedish folk ballads, and he suggested that his falling in love with the actress Harriet Bosse was the catalyst:

> Under Maeterlinck's influence then, and borrowing his divining rod, I searched in . . . sources. . . . There were princes and princesses to excess. I had already discovered the stepmother motif as a constant (in twenty-six Swedish folktales); awakening from death was there. . . . So I put everything into the separator with maidens and the Green Gardener and the young king, and so the cream was tossed out, and in this way it has become mine!
>
> But it's mine, too, because I've lived that tale in my fantasy! One spring, during the winter! (p. 305)

In a letter (May 5, 1908) to the actress Anna Flygare, he made his intention in the play clear:

> Eros is not the major motif; it [the play] symbolizes only Caritas, the great Love, which suffers everything, which forgives, hopes, believes, even when everything has let one down; expressed even better in the Stepmother's change in character—best in the final scene: Love [is] stronger than Death!—Rather the spirit of love in mind and heart than in beautiful form and external charms.

He intended then to compose a folktale in drama form, a folktale play (*ett sagospel*) that would approach in content and form a marionette play. In his mood at that time he thought of *Swanwhite* as a dramatized hymn to love—a love, he insisted, in which pure or spiritual love dominates over physical, sexual love. *Swanwhite* was not intended to be either a naturalistic-realistic drama or a dreamplay, but a play which requires a child's response or the willing suspension of disbelief—a play for children of all ages, a play that would combine entertainment and instruction.

The plot is simple. The daughter of a medieval duke is persecuted by her wicked stepmother, falls in love with and is loved by a young prince, is courted by a sensual young king, loses her prince through drowning, but, through her love, her purity, and her mercy, succeeds in having him restored to life.

Strindberg thought of the Middle Ages as an age of faith, of myth, of imagination, and of antitheses (good–evil, black–white, false–true). In his view, those ages were childlike, that is, man was not handicapped by obsessive analysis of the harsh realities of earthly life, but was able to escape through imagination and faith into states of ecstasy in which miracles, wonders, and magic were not only possible, but probable. It is the spirit of a time so conceived that Strindberg has caught.

Detailed as the stage set may seem at first reading, it is strikingly different from that of, say, *Lady Julie*, in which every item of stage property, was to be exactly in keeping with a Swedish manor house of the 1880s. The set is stylized, but instead of realistic reproduction or presentation of actuality, Strindberg's set is designed to produce an effect, to suggest the color and the atmosphere of ornate medieval trappings.

The characters are "stylized" as well. They are not

analyzed in depth, but rather are synthetic types of the kind one finds in folktales. They are anything but carefully presented case reports, being closer to figures such as The Hunter and The Child in *The Great Highway*. Swanwhite herself is an embodiment of early youth, goodness, beauty, innocence, and young love, childlike in her need to be entertained and to entertain, willing to learn, and supplied only with minor flaws that training can eliminate. The prince is her male counterpart, endowed richly in admirable physical, emotional, and intellectual features and dedicated to observation of the chivalric code of conduct. The duke is a heroic knight, a defender of good against evil.

Contrasted to these three in the cast of black or white figures are the wicked stepmother and the sensual young king, both of whom are, however, conceived of as evil only because of factors beyond their control. The stepmother with her typically folktale props—the steel whip, the nails on the floor, bloodhounds, magic mirror, evil tongue, and pantherlike walk—is evil only because of what misfortune has meted out to her: the death of the man she loved. Love alone can restore her from her troll state to being the good person she is by nature. She shares that sentimental notion that all human beings are by nature good—a notion Strindberg rarely entertained—with the young king who can rise to moral behavior: "forgive me for what I have done, forget I have existed and never think I'd dare to touch you with an impure thought; your memory alone shall pursue me and punish me. . . ." He does revert to ugly behavior, but the implication is clear. He, too, can be a worthy human being.

Signe, Elsa, and Tova, the three girls who serve as Swanwhite's attendants and as the guardians of the three rooms, share with the gardeners, the officials, the knights, and the servants roles as puppets going through their designated paces as the person in power manipulates the strings. Note the rare deviations from doll-like behavior by the three maids, and note, too, the marionettelike procession of the servants.

Magic and miracle are elements in folk literature and in the children's literature of Strindberg's day and beyond. Thus the appearance of the two dead mothers with their magic means of transport and the sensitive response of the peacock and the birds to the slightest hint of unacceptable behavior should disturb neither the child who is still childlike nor the adult who has suspended disbelief. All these matters—even, appreciably, the dialog—can be delightful matters for children and delightful demonstrations to adults of Strindberg's knowledge of and control over the elements of the folktale and the spirit of folk literature.

But *Swanwhite* is far more explicit than most folktales on matters that always caused Strindberg concern. The play does scrutinize evil and more than suggests means of coping with it. Consider, for example, the unfortunate family situation (father vs. stepmother, stepdaughter vs. stepmother, father and daughter vs. stepmother). The solutions in this play are different from those in his other plays, of course; for once, the dramatist was in a mood to permit the family members to be reconciled through the magic of love and to allow his play to end very happily indeed.

Strindberg did have difficulty on occasion in presenting the very young in his dramas and his prose fiction. While he had some remnants of the romantic notion of children's "innocence" and their capacity for sensing and seeing into the truth about the people and the world about them, he knew very well the need for training and discipline of the young. His reluctance about "touching the butterfly's wings," as he puts it in *Easter,* may help explain why his presentation of the very young does strike many adult readers as disturbingly cloying.

Be that as it may, *Swanwhite* has been successfully produced on the Swedish stage time and again. Some of Sweden's well-known actresses have created the role of Swanwhite: among them Fanny Falkner, the girl who turned down chances to become Strindberg's fourth wife, and Tora Teje and Inga Tidblad, both among the greatest actresses Sweden has had.

'Swanwhite'

'Characters'

THE YOUNG KING
THE DUKE
THE STEPMOTHER
SWANWHITE
THE PRINCE
SIGNE ⎫
ELSA ⎬ MAIDS
TOVA ⎭
THE GARDENER
THE FISHERMAN

SWANWHITE'S MOTHER
THE PRINCE'S MOTHER
THE EXECUTIONER
THE SHERIFF
THE STEWARD
THE HERB GARDENER
KNIGHT I
KNIGHT II
Minor characters

Settings *(for the whole play)*

An apartment in a meaieval stone castle. The walls and ceiling are completely white; the roof is cross-vaulted. In the back center a doorway in three arches opening onto a stone porch. The doorway can be closed with brocade drapes. Below the porch the back shows the top of a rose tree grove, tall rose trees with pink and white roses. Beyond can be seen a white sandy beach and the blue sea.

To the right of the doorway is a little door, which when it is open, shows the perspective of three rooms, opening into each other. In the first, which is the Pewter Room, pewter vessels are on shelves. In the second, the Clothes Room, beautiful garments can be seen. In the third, the

Fruit Room, can be seen apples, pears, pumpkins, and melons.

The floor in all the rooms are checked, red and black. In the middle of the apartment is a gilded dining table with a cloth, two gilded chairs, a clock, and a vase with roses in it. Mistletoe is suspended over the table. A lionskin lies on the floor in the foreground. Two swallows' nests are just over the small doorway. To the front left is a white bed with a rose-colored canopy supported by two posts at the head (there are no posts at the foot). The bed has white bedclothes except that the coverlet is extremely pale blue silk. On it lies a sheer white nightgown with lace. Back of the bed is a wall cupboard for towels, linen, etc. Beside the bed is a small gilded Roman table (round on a column) and a lampstand on which is a Roman lamp of gold. To the right is a beautifully sculptured stove, on which is a vase with a white lily in it.

In the left arch of the doorway a peacock is sleeping on a perch with his back to the audience.

In the right arch is a large golden cage with two white doves at rest.

ACT I

When the curtain goes up, the audience can see the three MAIDS, *one in each of the three chamber doors but half-concealed by the doorposts. The false attendant,* SIGNE, *stands in the Pewter Room doorway;* ELSA, *in the Clothes Room;* TOVA, *in the Fruit Room.*

The DUKE *enters from the back; then the* STEPMOTHER *with a steel whip in her hand.*

The stage is dim when they enter.

The sound of bugles.

STEPMOTHER (*looks about*): Swanwhite isn't here?

DUKE: It looks like it!

STEPMOTHER: It *does,* but I can't see her. Girls! . . . Signe! Elsa! Tova! . . . (*The* MAIDS *come in in a row, the one behind the other and stop before the* STEPMOTHER.) Where is Lady Swanwhite?

(SIGNE *crosses her arms over her chest, says nothing.*)

STEPMOTHER: Don't know? (*Shakes the steel whip.*) What do you see in my hand? . . . Answer quickly!

(SIGNE *remains silent.*)

STEPMOTHER: Quickly! (*Cracks the whip loudly.*) Hear how the falcon whistles; it has claws of steel, and a beak! What *is* it?

SIGNE: The steel whip!

STEPMOTHER: Yes, it's the steel whip! So where is Lady Swanwhite?

SIGNE: I can't say what I don't know!

STEPMOTHER: Ignorance is a vice, but ingratitude's a flaw!
Weren't you supposed to keep an eye on your young lady
. . . Take off your neckcloth! . . .
(SIGNE, *in despair, loosens her neckcloth*.)
STEPMOTHER: On your knees!
(*The* DUKE *turns his back in disgust.*)
STEPMOTHER: Bend your neck! And I'll put a collar on it so
no young swain will be able to kiss it any more! . . . Bend
your neck! Still more!
SIGNE: Mercy, for the Lord's sake!
STEPMOTHER: I've already given you mercy in letting you
keep your life!
DUKE (*draws his sword and tries its edge on his nail and then on
his long beard. Ambiguously*): The head should be off; be
stuffed in a sack; be hung in a tree . . .
STEPMOTHER: Yes, it should!
DUKE: We agree! Imagine!
STEPMOTHER: We didn't yesterday!
DUKE: Probably not tomorrow!
STEPMOTHER (*to* SIGNE, *who on her knees has moved away*):
Stop! Where are you going? (*Lifts the steel whip and strikes.*
SIGNE *moves so that the whip whistles in the air.*)

*

SWANWHITE (*crawls on her knees out from the other side of the
bed*): Stepmother! Here I am! the guilty one; Signe is
innocent!
STEPMOTHER: Say Mother! Say Mother, first!
SWANWHITE: I can't! A human being has only one mother!
STEPMOTHER: Your father's wife is your mother!
SWANWHITE: My father's second wife is my stepmother!
STEPMOTHER: You're stubborn, but the steel's pliable and will
make you pliable! (*Raises her whip toward* SWANWHITE.)
DUKE (*raises his sword*): Watch the head!
STEPMOTHER: Which one?

DUKE: Yours!

STEPMOTHER (*turns pale; becomes angry, then calm and silent. A long pause. Then, defeated, turns to the* DUKE): So: You will now tell your daughter what's ahead of her!

DUKE (*puts up his sword*): Dear child, get up, and calm yourself in my arms!

SWANWHITE (*leaps into the* DUKE'*s arms*): Father! . . . You're like a royal oak, and I can't embrace you; but under your foliage I'll hide myself from unkind showers . . . (*She conceals her head under his huge beard, which covers him down to his waist.*) And on your branches I'll rock like a bird . . . lift me up, so I can climb in the crown! (*The* DUKE *extends his arm;* SWANWHITE *climbs up on his shoulder.*) Now I have the earth under me and the air over, now I see out over the rose garden, the white sandy shore, the blue sea and seven kingdoms!

DUKE: Then you see the young king, your betrothed,[1] too . . .

SWANWHITE: No, and I've never seen him . . . Is he handsome?

DUKE: Dear heart . . . It depends on your eyes how you see him!

SWANWHITE (*rubs her eyes*): My eyes? . . . They see only what's beautiful!

DUKE (*kisses her foot*): My little foot, which is very black! A black little foot!

(*The* STEPMOTHER *has signaled to the* MAIDS, *who resume their places in the doorways. She herself steals out through the door at the back like a panther.*)

*

SWANWHITE (*jumps down; the* DUKE *puts her on the table and sits down on a chair next to the table.* SWANWHITE *looks meaningfully toward her* STEPMOTHER): Did the sun rise? Did the wind turn southerly? Has spring come? . . .

DUKE (*places his hand over her mouth*): Little chatterbox! Joy of
my old age; star of the evening of my life! Open your
rosy-red ear and close your little seashell of a mouth. . . .
Listen carefully! Obey me, and it will go well for you! . . .

SWANWHITE (*sticks her fingers in her ears*): I hear with my eyes,
I see with my ears. . . Now I see nothing, only hear!

DUKE: Child! . . . In your cradle you were betrothed to the
young king of Rigalid. You have never seen him, because
it's not in keeping with court etiquette. The day when the
sacred bonds are to be tied is approaching. To teach you
courtly manners and the duties of queen, the king has sent
a young prince, with whom you're to learn to read, to play
chess, to dance, and to play the harp.

SWANWHITE: What's the prince's name?

DUKE: Well, my child, you mayn't ask that from him or
anyone else: because it has been foretold: the one who can
call him by name has to love him!

SWANWHITE: Is he handsome?

DUKE: Yes; since you see *only* beauty.

SWANWHITE: But the prince is handsome?

DUKE: Yes, he is! Watch out for your little heart which
belongs to the king, and never forget you were a queen
even in your cradle . . . And so, my child, I leave you, for
I have to go to war! . . . Be humble and obedient to your
stepmother; she is a hard woman, but your father has loved
her, and a gentle spirit can break open a heart of stone. If
her wickedness should surpass the limits of the permissible
in spite of her promises and vows, blow this horn—(*He
takes a sculptured ebony horn from under his cloak*)—and
you'll get help. But don't blow it before you have to,
before your need is extreme! . . . Understand?

SWANWHITE: And?

DUKE: Well then: the prince is already here, down in the
reception room. Do you want to see him now?

SWANWHITE: *Do* I want to?

DUKE: Shall I first say good-bye?

SWANWHITE: Is the prince already here?

DUKE: He's already here, I'm already—there, far away, where the heron of forgetfulness[2] sticks his head under his wing!

SWANWHITE (*leaps up on the* DUKE*'s lap and hides her head under his beard*): Don't say that, don't say that! I'm ashamed!

DUKE: My little darling should get a spanking for so quickly forgetting her old father because of a young prince! Shame! (*A bugle sounds in the distance.*)

DUKE (*gets up hastily; takes* SWANWHITE *in his arms, throws her up in the air and catches her*): Little bird, fly, keep yourself high above the dirt and always have air under your wings! . . There! Down to earth! . . . Honor and war summon me! . . . Love and youth, you. (*Girds himself with his sword.*) And now hide your miracle horn so that wicked eyes don't see it!

SWANWHITE: Where shall I hide it? Where?

DUKE: In your bed!

SWANWHITE (*hides the horn under the bedding*): Sleep there! Sleep well, little tooter! When the time comes, I'll awaken you! Don't forget to say your evening prayers!

DUKE: Child! Don't forget my last wish: Obey your stepmother!

SWANWHITE: In everything?

DUKE: In everything!

SWANWHITE: Not in what is dirty! . . . My mother gave me two changes in linen every eight days: this one gives me one! Mother gave me water and soap, Stepmother won't give me any! Just look at my poor little feet!

DUKE: Daughter, keep yourself clean inwardly and the outward will become clean. Did you know that holy men who as a penance may not use cleansing water become white as swans, but unholy ones get black as ravens!

SWANWHITE: Then I want to become that white! . . .

DUKE: Let me hug you! And so good-bye!

SWANWHITE (*leaps into his arms*): Good-bye, great hero in battle, wonderful father! May you be blessed in years, in friends, in victories!

DUKE: May your loving prayers protect me! (*Lowers the vizier on his golden helmet.*)

SWANWHITE (*jumps up and kisses the vizier*): The golden portals are shut, but I see your friendly protective eye through the bars. (*She knocks on the vizier.*) Open up, open up, for a little red top . . . No one at home. "Come see!" said the wolf, who was lying in the bed!

DUKE (*puts her down on the floor*): Lovely flower; grow and be fragrant! If I come back, fine, I come; if not, my eye shall watch over you from the starry vault above and I shall never cease to see you, for up there one becomes all-seeing as the creative God!
(*Goes firmly with a gesture for her to stay.*)

(SWANWHITE *kneels and prays for the* DUKE. *All the rose trees sway in the wind which sighs outside. The peacock shakes his wings and tail feathers.*)

SWANWHITE (*gets up; goes up to the peacock and pats him on the back and tail*): Pavo, dear Pavo! What do you see? What do you hear? Is someone coming? Who's coming? Is it a little prince? Is he handsome and kind? You can see that with your many blue eyes? (*She lifts a tail feather and looks at its eyes.*)
Are you going to keep your eyes on us, wicked Argus?[3] Are you going to see to it two young human beings' little hearts don't beat too loudly . . . You fool! I'll pull the curtain, you see . . . (*She draws a curtain which conceals the*

peacock, but not the landscape outside. Then she goes up to the doves.)

My white doves, white, white, white, you are going to see the whitest of all . . . Be still, wind; be still, roses; be still, doves, my prince is coming!

(She looks out, then withdraws to the Pewter Room door which she leaves open a little so she can observe the PRINCE *through the crack. She remains standing there, visible to the audience but unseen by the* PRINCE.*)*

*

PRINCE *(enters through the archway at the back. He is dressed in black and in steel armor. After he has carefully observed all the things in the room, he sits down at the table, takes off his helmet and looks at it. He now turns his back to the door, back of which* SWANWHITE *stands concealed):* If someone is here, let him speak up! *(Silence)* There is someone in here, for I can feel the warmth in a young body billow against me like a south wind; I hear breath fragrant as roses, and weak as it is it makes the feather on my helmet move. *(He puts the helmet to his ear.)* My helmet sighs like a big seashell; that's my thoughts collecting themselves like a swarm of bees in a log. Buz-z! buz-z! say my thoughts . . . just like bees, and they buzz about the queen . . . the little queen of my thoughts, of my dreams! *(He puts the helmet in front of himself on the table and observes it.)* Dark and arched as the night sky, but without stars, for the black feather makes everything black since my mother died . . . *(He turns the helmet about and looks at it.)* But there, in the darkness, far down . . . on the other side I see a ray of light . . . have the heavens been rent . . . and in the ray I see . . . not a star, for that looks like a diamond, but a blue sapphire, the queen of gems, the blue of the summer sky, in a milky white cloud, arched like a dove's egg . . . What is it? Is it

my ring? And a velvet black feathery cloud draws by . . .
and the sapphire smiles, but the sapphire can't smile . . .
now there's lightning, but it's blue! . . . heat lightning,
warm without peals . . . What are you? Who are you?
Where are you? (*He looks at the back of the helmet.*) Not
there! Not here! Nowhere! (*He lowers his face to the helmet.*)
I approach, and you retreat!

 (SWANWHITE *steals forward on her toes.*)
Now they're two! . . . Two eyes! . . . Small human eyes
. . . I kiss you! (*He kisses the helmet.*)

     *

SWANWHITE (*comes up to the table and sits down, slowly, directly
 across from the* PRINCE. *He gets up, bows as he puts his hand
 over his heart and observes* SWANWHITE): Are you the little
 prince?
PRINCE: The young king's faithful servant, and yours!
SWANWHITE: What does the young king say to his bride?
PRINCE: He greets Lady Swanwhite with a thousand loving
 greetings, and says that the delightful happiness which
 awaits him will shorten the long agony of longing.
SWANWHITE (*who has been studying the* PRINCE *searchingly*):
 Why don't you sit down, my prince?
PRINCE: If I were to sit while you sit, I'd have to kneel if you
 were standing!
SWANWHITE: Tell me about the king! About his looks!
PRINCE: What he looks like! (*Puts a hand over his eyes*)
 Strange! I can't see him any more!
SWANWHITE: What do you mean?
PRINCE: He's gone; he's invisible . . .
SWANWHITE: Is he tall?
PRINCE (*fixes* SWANWHITE's *glance*): Wait! . . . Now I see
 him! . . . Taller than you!
SWANWHITE: Handsome?
PRINCE: Can't compare with you!

SWANWHITE: Talk about the king, not about me!

PRINCE: I am talking about the king!

SWANWHITE: Is he fair or dark?

PRINCE: If he were dark and saw you, he'd become fair at once.

SWANWHITE: That's more polite than sensible! Are his eyes blue?

PRINCE (*looks at the helmet*): Don't I have to take a look?

SWANWHITE (*holds up her hand between them*): You! You!

PRINCE: Y-O-U, Y-O-U—

SWANWHITE: Are you going to teach me the alphabet?

PRINCE: The young king is a tall blond man with blue eyes, broad shoulders, masses of hair . . .

SWANWHITE: Why do you wear a black feather?

PRINCE: His lips are red as cloudberries, his cheeks white and a young lion wouldn't be ashamed of having teeth like his!

SWANWHITE: Why is your hair wet?

PRINCE: His mind knows no fear and his heart has never borne anguish because of a wicked deed!

SWANWHITE: Why is your hand trembling?

PRINCE: We should talk about the young king and not about me!

SWANWHITE: You, you want to teach me?

PRINCE: It's my duty, milady, to teach you to love the young king, whose throne you will share!

SWANWHITE: How did you cross the sea to get here?

PRINCE: With sail and sailboat!

SWANWHITE: In the wind!

PRINCE: One can't sail without wind.

SWANWHITE: How wise you are! . . . Do you want to play games with me?

PRINCE: I want to do my duty!

SWANWHITE: Now you're going to see what I have in my chest. (*She goes up to the chest, kneels, takes out dolls, a rattle, and a hobbyhorse.*) There's the doll . . . that's my child, my child of sorrow, who can never keep her face clean . . . I've taken her down into the wash house and scrubbed her with white sand . . . but she only got dirtier . . . I've spanked her, but that doesn't help . . . now I've thought of the worst possible!

PRINCE: And what would that be?

SWANWHITE (*looks about*): She's going to get a stepmother!

PRINCE: But how can that be? She has to have a mother first!

SWANWHITE: Well, I'm her mother, and if I remarry, I'll be a stepmother!

PRINCE: No, no, no! It doesn't work that way!

SWANWHITE: And you'll be the stepfather!

PRINCE: Oh no!

SWANWHITE: But you're to be good to her even though she can't wash her face. . . . Take her, so I can see if you can hold a child!

(*The* PRINCE *unwillingly takes the doll.*)

SWANWHITE: You can't yet, but you're going to learn! Take the rattle, and shake it for her!

(*The* PRINCE *takes the rattle.*)

SWANWHITE: You don't know how, I see! (*Takes the doll and the rattle and tosses them into the chest. Then she picks up the hobbyhorse.*) Here's my charger. . . . He has a golden saddle and silver shoes. . . . He can run seven miles an hour, and on him I've ridden through the Heard Forest, over the Great Heath, on the King's Bridge, the Great Highway, the Avenue of Anxiety, up to the Sea of Tears! And there he lost a golden shoe that fell into the lake, and a fish came, and then a fisherman, and then I got the golden shoe back. Now we know that! (*Tosses the hobbyhorse into the chest. Picks up a chessboard with white and red squares and gold and silver pieces.*) If you want to play chess with me, sit down there on the lion skin! (*She sits down on the lionskin and sets up the pieces.*) Sit down—the girls won't see us here! (*Embarrassed, the* PRINCE *sits down on the hide.*)

SWANWHITE (*runs her hand through the lionskin's hair and mane*): This is like sitting in grass, not the green meadow's but the desert's that the sun has scorched. . . . Now say something, about me! Do you like me a little?

PRINCE: Shall we play chess?

SWANWHITE: Play chess? What do I care about that? . . . (*Sighs*) . . . You're to teach me something!

PRINCE: What do I, poor soul, know besides saddling a horse or bearing weapons? And that wouldn't do you any good.

SWANWHITE: Are you sad?

PRINCE: My mother is dead.

SWANWHITE: Poor prince! . . . My mother's with God in heaven, too, and has become an angel. Sometimes I see her at night. Do you see yours?

PRINCE: No-o-!

SWANWHITE: Do you have a stepmother?

PRINCE: Not yet; my mother passed away only a short time ago.

SWANWHITE: Don't be so sad. . . . Everything goes over, you see. Now I'm going to give you a flag so you'll be happy again. . . . But I did sew this one for the young king; I'll sew one for you! . . The king's is this one with the seven bonfires. . . . I'll give you one with seven red roses . . . but you're to hold the skein for me first. . . . (*She picks up a skein of rosy-red yarn from the chest and hands it to the* PRINCE.) One, two, three! I'll begin now, but your hand mustn't shake! . . . Maybe you want a hair of mine in the yarn! . . . Pull one out!

PRINCE: No, no, I couldn't. . . .

SWANWHITE: Then I will! (*She tears out a hair and weaves it into the yarn.*) What is your name?

PRINCE: You're not supposed to ask!

SWANWHITE: Why not?

PRINCE: Didn't the duke tell you?

SWANWHITE: No! What could happen if a person said his name? Could something dangerous happen?

PRINCE: Didn't the duke say?

SWANWHITE: I've never heard the like, not being allowed to say his name. (*The curtain, back of which the peacock sits, now moves, and one can hear a vague sound as of castanets.*)

PRINCE (*listens intently*): What was that?

SWANWHITE (*uneasy*): That's Pavo! . . . Do you think he understands what we're saying?

PRINCE: Who knows?

SWANWHITE: Well, what is your name? (*The peacock snaps with his beak again.*)

PRINCE: I'm afraid—don't ask me again!

SWANWHITE: He's only snapping with his beak. . . . Keep your hands still! . . . Have you heard the story of the little princess who wasn't allowed to say the prince's name, because something would happen if she did? You know what? (*The curtain which has concealed the peacock is drawn to the side and the peacock has turned spreading his tail so that all his "eyes" seem to observe* SWANWHITE *and the* PRINCE.)

PRINCE: Who drew back the curtain? Who told the bird to watch us with his hundred eyes? . . . Don't ask me again!

SWANWHITE: Maybe it's true! . . . Lie down, Pavo! There! (*The curtain is drawn shut again.*)

PRINCE: Are there ghosts here?

SWANWHITE: You mean things like that—happen? . . . Well, a lot of things happen here; but I'm used to it! And besides . . . (*softly*) they say my stepmother is a witch! . . . There, I stuck my finger!

PRINCE: On what?

SWANWHITE: There was a splinter in the wool! The sheep

have been in the barn all winter . . . then things like that
happen! . . . Can you pull out the splinter?

PRINCE: Yes, but then we have to sit down at the table so we
can see. (*They get up, then sit down at the table.*)

SWANWHITE (*extends her little finger*): Do you see anything?

PRINCE (*somewhat more daring than before*): What I see? I can
see through your hand which is red inside; I see life and
the world in rose color . . .

SWANWHITE: Pull out the splinter! It hurts!

PRINCE: But I have to hurt you! . . . Forgive me before I do!

SWANWHITE: Yes, but help me then! . . .

PRINCE (*presses her little finger and pulls the splinter out with his
nails*): There's the nasty thing that dared to hurt you,
Swanwhite! (*Throws the splinter on the floor and pretends to
step on it.*)

SWANWHITE: Now you're to suck out blood, or it'll get
infected.

PRINCE (*does*): Now I drank your blood, now we're foster
brother and sister!

SWANWHITE: Brother and sister, yes, but weren't we that
right away? If not, why did you call me by my first name?

PRINCE: Did I?

SWANWHITE: Imagine, he didn't even notice! . . . Now I
have a little brother and that's you! . . . Brother dear!
Take my hand!

PRINCE (*takes her hand*): Sister dear! . . . (*Notices her pulse
under his thumb.*) What do you have there ticking away
. . . one, two, three, four . . . (*Continues counting silently
after he has looked at the watch.*)

SWANWHITE: Yes, what's that ticking? Always, always! The
heart's not in the finger, of course, but it's under one of my
breasts. . . . Feel, go ahead feel it! (*The doves move and coo
[warningly].*) What's wrong, my doves?

PRINCE: Sixty! Now I know what's ticking away . . . It's

Time! . . . Your little finger's the second hand, which has ticked sixty times when a minute has passed. Don't you think there's a heart in the watch?

SWANWHITE (*feeling the watch*): We can't get into the watch! Any more than into the heart! Feel my heart!

SIGNE (*comes in from the Pewter Room with a steel whip, that she puts down in the middle of the table*): The duchess commands that you're to sit on opposite sides of the table!

(*The* PRINCE *gets up, sits down directly across from* SWANWHITE. *They look at each other without saying anything for a while*).

SWANWHITE: We've come far from each other, yet we're still closer.

PRINCE: People are never closer than when they're apart!

SWANWHITE: And you know that?

PRINCE: I just learned it!

SWANWHITE: Now you're starting to teach me!

PRINCE: And you me!

SWANWHITE (*pointing at the fruit bowl*): Won't you have some fruit?

PRINCE: No, eating's so ugly!

SWANWHITE: Yes, it is!

PRINCE: There are three maids standing there, one in the Pewter Room, one in the Clothes Room, one in the Fruit Room. . . . Why are they standing there?

SWANWHITE: To keep an eye on us! . . . So that we don't do something forbidden!

PRINCE: Mayn't we walk in the rose garden?

SWANWHITE: I may walk in the rose garden only in the morning, for Stepmother's bloodhounds are there after that. I never get permission to go to the beach . . . that's why I can never bathe.

PRINCE: Have you never been on the beach, never heard the sea wash the sand?

SWANWHITE: Never! From here I can hear only the thunder of the waves when there's a storm. . . .

PRINCE: Haven't you heard the sighing of the wind when it blows over the waters?

SWANWHITE: No, it doesn't come this far.

PRINCE (*pushes the helmet over to* SWANWHITE): Listen to this and you'll hear it!

SWANWHITE (*puts the helmet to her ear*): What is it I'm hearing?

PRINCE: The song of the sea, the whisper of the wind. . . .

SWANWHITE: Really? I hear human voices. . . . Sh-h! . . . It's Stepmother talking! . . . She's talking to the steward! . . . She's talking about me . . . and the young king! . . . She's using wicked words . . . she swears I'll never be queen . . . and she swears . . . that . . . you . . . are going . . . to marry . . . her daughter . . . the wicked Lena. . . .

PRINCE: Honestly! . . . Can you hear that in the helmet?

SWANWHITE: Yes!

PRINCE: I didn't know you could! But I got it as a christening gift from my godmother!

SWANWHITE: Will you give me a feather?

PRINCE: Of course I will!

SWANWHITE: But you're to cut it so I can write with it!

PRINCE: You can write?

SWANWHITE: Father taught me . . . (*The* PRINCE *jerks a black feather out of the helmet, takes a silverhandled knife from his belt and forms the pen.* SWANWHITE *takes an inkwell and parchment from the table drawer.*)

PRINCE: Who is Lady Lena?

SWANWHITE (*writes*): What she is? Do you want her?

PRINCE: They're up to evil in this house! . . .

SWANWHITE: Fear nothing! Father has given me a gift which in the hour of need will bring help!

PRINCE: What's it called?

SWANWHITE: It's the horn Stand-by!

PRINCE: Where's it kept?

SWANWHITE: Read that in my eyes! I don't dare to tell you aloud because of the maids!

PRINCE (*looks into her eyes*): I see it!

SWANWHITE (*pushes the ink, pen, and parchment over to him*): Write! (*The PRINCE writes.*) Yes, it's there! (*Writes again*).

PRINCE: What are you writing?

SWANWHITE: Names! All the attractive names for princes!

PRINCE: Except mine!

SWANWHITE: Yours, too!

PRINCE: Don't!

SWANWHITE: Now I've written twenty names, all I know, and now your name's there, too. (*Pushes her parchment over to him.*) Read it! (*The PRINCE reads it. SWANWHITE claps her hands.*) Ah, I read it in your eyes!

PRINCE: Don't say it! By all that's merciful, don't say it!

SWANWHITE: I read it in your eyes!

PRINCE: But don't say it! Don't say it!

SWANWHITE: Why not? What would happen? . . . Is Lena to say it? Your bride! The girl you love!

PRINCE: Sh-h! Hush!

SWANWHITE (*has got up; dances about*): I know your name, the loveliest name in all the world!

(*The PRINCE gets up, catches her, and puts his hand over her mouth.*)

SWANWHITE: Now I'll bite your hand, I'll suck your blood, we'll be brother and sister twice over. Do you know what that means?

PRINCE: Brother and sister!

SWANWHITE (*tosses her head back*): Ah, ha! There's a hole in the ceiling and I see the heavens, a little bit of the heavens, a pane, and back of the pane is a face. Is it an angel's . . . No, but look, look! . . . It's your face!

PRINCE: Angels are little girls, not boys!

SWANWHITE: But it is you!

PRINCE (*looks up at the ceiling*): It's a mirror!

SWANWHITE (*sighs*): It's Stepmother's magic mirror. She has seen everything.

PRINCE: And in the mirror I see the hearth and in the hearth a pumpkin is hanging!

SWANWHITE (*takes a multicolored, strangely shaped pumpkin out of the fireplace*): What is this? It looks like an ear! . . . The witch has heard us, too! . . . (*Sighs. Throws the pumpkin into the fire. Runs to the bed; stops suddenly and raises one foot.*) She has put needles on the floor. . . . (*Sits down and rubs her foot.*)

(*The* PRINCE *kneels before* SWANWHITE *to help her.*)

SWANWHITE: No, no, you mayn't touch my foot! You mayn't!

PRINCE: Dear heart, you have to get your stocking off if I'm to help!

SWANWHITE (*sobs*): You mayn't, you may not see my foot!

PRINCE: But why not, why not?

SWANWHITE (*drawing her foot under her*): I can't tell you, I can't. Leave me, leave me! . . . I'll tell you tomorrow! I can't today! . . .

PRINCE: But your little foot is hurting: I must pull out the needle!

SWANWHITE: Go, go, go. . . . Oh no, you mayn't! . . . If my mother were alive, this would never have happened! Mother, mother, mother!

PRINCE: I don't understand . . . are you afraid of me . . .

SWANWHITE: Don't ask! . . . Just leave me! (*Sobs.*)

PRINCE (*upset; gets up*): What have I done?

SWANWHITE: Don't leave me! . . . I didn't want to hurt you! . . . But I can't tell you. . . . If I could get to the beach, into the white sand . . .

PRINCE: What then?

SWANWHITE: I can't tell you! I can't! (*Hides her face in her hands.*)

(*Now the peacock snaps his beak; the doves become restless. The three* MAIDS *march in a row; a puff of wind and the rustling of the trees in the rose garden can be heard; golden-tinted clouds over the sea float to the side; the blue sea itself darkens.*)

SWANWHITE (*who has noticed what has been happening*): Is Heaven sitting in judgment over us? . . . Has misfortune come to this house? . . . Oh, if I could only mourn my mother out of the black earth!

PRINCE (*puts his hand on his sword*): For you—I'd give my life!

SWANWHITE: No, no—she deafens swords, too! . . . If I could only mourn my mother out of the black earth! (*The swallows twitter in their nests.*) What was that?

PRINCE (*notices the swallows' nest*): A swallows' nest! I didn't see that before!

SWANWHITE: I didn't either! How did that get there? When did it get there? . . . Doesn't matter, it's a good sign. . . . But I'm perspiring with anxiety . . . and it's as if I were choking. . . . You see, even the rose over there starts to wither when that wicked woman approaches . . . for it's she who's coming. . . . (*The rose on the table has begun to close and its leaves hang.*)

PRINCE: But the swallows! Where did they come from?

SWANWHITE: Certainly not from that wicked woman, for swallows are good birds. . . . Now she's here!

*

STEPMOTHER (*strides in like a panther from the back. The rose collapses on the table.*): Signe! . . . Take the horn out of the bed!

(SIGNE *goes up to the bed and takes the horn.*)

STEPMOTHER: Prince, where do you intend to go?

PRINCE: Duchess, it's getting late, the sun's setting, and my boat wants to get home!

STEPMOTHER: It's too late, the gates have been closed, and the dogs let out. . . . Do you know about my dogs?

PRINCE: Yes, indeed! But do you know about my sword?

STEPMOTHER: Is there something special about that sword?

PRINCE: Blood, now and then!

STEPMOTHER: Ah ha! . . . Never woman's blood surely? Listen, do you want to sleep in the Blue Room, Prince?

PRINCE: No, by my faith, I want to sleep at home in my own bed!

STEPMOTHER: Are there others who want that?

PRINCE: Many!

STEPMOTHER: How many? . . . This many? . . . One! Two!

(*As she counts, a procession of the people on the estate starts going by on the veranda, all of them serious, some armed, and without looking into the room. The* STEWARD, *the* HEAD COOK, *the* EXECUTIONER, *the* STABLEMASTER, *the* GROOM, *etc.*)

PRINCE (*having observed the procession*): I'll sleep in the Blue Room!

STEPMOTHER: I thought so! . . . Then I'll say good-night to Your Royal Highness . . . Swanwhite will, too, of course!

(*A swan flies past outside the rose garden; a poppy falls from the roof onto the* STEPMOTHER *who falls asleep along with the three* MAIDS.)

SWANWHITE (*comes up to the* PRINCE): Good night, Prince!
. . .

PRINCE (*takes her hand and says softly*): Good night! . . . If I may only sleep under the same roof as my princess, my dreams will embrace your dreams, and tomorrow we'll get up to play new games, new ones. . . .

SWANWHITE (*softly*): Now you're everything to me, you're my father. . . . Since she has taken his mighty support away from me. See, she's sleeping!

PRINCE: Did you see the swan?

SWANWHITE: No, but I heard her! It was my mother!

PRINCE: Flee with me!

SWANWHITE: No, we mayn't! . . . Patience! We'll meet in our dreams! Isn't that right? . . . But so we can, you have to . . . like me more than everything else on earth! Like me, really like me!

PRINCE: My king and my faith . . .

SWANWHITE: Your queen and your heart . . . I am both!

PRINCE: I am a knight!

SWANWHITE: I'm not! And so: so I take you . . . Prince . . . (*She cups her hands over her mouth and "throws" his name out in a whisper.*)

PRINCE: Alas, what did you do?

SWANWHITE: You got me in your name, you got yourself back with me on *your* wings! You . . . (*whispers his name again*).

PRINCE (*as if he were catching the name in the air with one hand*): Was it a rose you threw to me? (*He kisses one finger and throws it back.*) Swanwhite!

SWANWHITE: You gave me a violet! That's you! It's your soul! Now I'll drink you; now I have you in my heart, now you're mine!

PRINCE: And you're mine! Who then is the owner?

SWANWHITE: We!

PRINCE: You and I! . . . my Rose!

SWANWHITE: My Violet!

PRINCE: Rose!

SWANWHITE: Violet!

PRINCE: I love you!

SWANWHITE: You love me!

PRINCE: You love me!

SWANWHITE: I love you!

(*The stage turns light. The rose on the table rises and opens. The faces of the* STEPMOTHER *and the three* MAIDS *glow with expressions of beauty, goodness, and happiness. The* STEPMOTHER'*s sleep-heavy head is raised and with closed eyes she seems to observe the young people's happiness with a sunny smile.*)

SWANWHITE: Look, look at her! The cruel woman's smiling as if she were remembering happiness in her youth; false Signe is pure faithfulness and hope; ugly Tova is beautiful; and little Elsa has grown!

PRINCE: It's our love that has done that!

SWANWHITE: Is it our love? Thanks be to God, mighty creative God! (*She falls to her knees and weeps.*)

PRINCE: Are you weeping?

SWANWHITE: Yes, because I'm happy!

PRINCE: Let me embrace you, then you'd smile!

SWANWHITE: In your embrace, I'd die!

PRINCE: Smile and die!

SWANWHITE (*gets up*): Let me die!

(*The* PRINCE *takes her in his arms.*)

*

STEPMOTHER (*awakens, strikes the table with the steel whip when she sees the young couple*): I think I've been sleeping! . . . Ah ha! So you've come to that! . . . Did I say the Blue Room? I meant the Blue Tower, where you're going to sleep, Prince! with the Iron Maiden![4] . . . Girls! (*The* MAIDS *wake up.*) Show the prince the direct way to the Blue Tower. And if he doesn't get there, call the steward, the executioner, the groom, the guard!

PRINCE: You don't need to! I may go into fire, into water, into earth, over the clouds, and I'd still meet my Swanwhite, for she's everywhere where I am! So now I'll go to meet her . . . in the Blue Tower. Can you do magic

like that, you troll? . . . Hardly! For you do not have love!
(*Goes, followed by the three* MAIDS.)

STEPMOTHER (*to* SWANWHITE): You won't need many words
. . . so say your wishes, quickly!

SWANWHITE: My first and greatest is clean water so I can wash
my feet!

STEPMOTHER: Cold or warm?

SWANWHITE: If I dare . . . warm.

STEPMOTHER: What else?

SWANWHITE: A comb to straighten my hair!

STEPMOTHER: Gold or silver?

SWANWHITE: Are you, are you good?

STEPMOTHER: Gold or silver?

SWANWHITE: Wooden or horn is good enough for me!

STEPMOTHER: What else?

SWANWHITE: Clean underclothes!

STEPMOTHER: Silk or linen?

SWANWHITE: Linen!

STEPMOTHER: Fine! Now I've heard your wishes. Listen to
mine! I wish that you will get no water, neither cold nor
warm! . . . I wish that you do not get any comb, neither
wooden nor horn, still less gold or silver, that's how good I
am! I wish that you may not wear linen but that you go into
the Clothes Room and put on the black homespun shift! I
have spoken! . . . And if you leave these rooms, which
you can't because I've set out traps, then you'll die, or I'll
mark up that pretty mug of yours with this steel whip, so
that neither princes nor kings would look at you again!
Now go to bed!

(*Strikes the table with the steel whip, gets up and goes to shut
the back door with golden gates which creak and squeak.*)

[CURTAIN]

ACT II

The same setting, but the golden gates are closed. The peacock and the doves are sleeping. The golden clouds are as dark as the sea and the land in the distance.

SWANWHITE is lying on the bed dressed in black homespun.

The doors to the Pewter Room, the Clothes Room, and the Fruit Room are open. The three MAIDS *stand motionless with closed eyes and holding small, burning Roman lamps in their hands.*

A swan flies past outside above the rose garden. A chord of trumpet notes can be heard reminiscent of migrating swans.

Then SWANWHITE'S *mother, dressed in white, appears outside the gates. She is carrying a swan-"guise"⁵ on one arm and a small golden harp on the other. She hangs the swanguise on the gate, which opens and closes of itself.*

The MOTHER *enters and puts the harp on the table. She looks about and notices* SWANWHITE. *Then the harp begins to play: the* MAIDS' *lamps go out one by one, the farthermost first, and the doors to the rooms close one by one, the farthermost first.*

The golden clouds regain their golden glow.

The MOTHER *lights a lamp on the lampstand and then kneels down.*

The harp continues playing during the scene that follows.

The MOTHER *gets up, picks up* SWANWHITE *and places her in the large armchair without awakening her. She kneels, takes off her daughter's stockings, and puts them under the bed, weeps as she bends over* SWANWHITE's *small feet as if she were moistening them with her tears; then she dries them with a white linen towel, and kisses them; puts pure white sandals on* SWANWHITE's *now white feet. The* MOTHER *gets up again, takes a golden comb, and combs* SWANWHITE's *hair. Then she carries the girl back to the bed and takes out of her bag a white garment which she spreads out beside* SWANWHITE. *She kisses her daughter on the forehead and prepares to leave. Then a white swan flies by outside and the same chord can be heard. Then the* PRINCE's MOTHER, *dressed in white, comes through the gate on which she hangs her "guise."*

SWANWHITE'S MOTHER: Well met, Sister! Are we near cock's crow?

PRINCE'S MOTHER: Pretty near! The dew's already rising from the roses; the corncrake can be heard in the hayfield, and the dawn's rising over the sea.

SWANWHITE'S MOTHER: Let's hurry to do what we must, Sister.

PRINCE'S MOTHER: You called me so we might talk about our children!

SWANWHITE'S MOTHER: I was walking in a green meadow in the land where there are no sorrows; there I met you for the first time, but I have always known you all the same . . . and you spoke with pity about your poor boy, who was alone in the valley of sorrow. . . . You opened my heart; and my thoughts, though unwilling to dwell down here, sought out my poor deserted girl . . . destined to be the wife of the young king, a cruel man and an evil one.

PRINCE'S MOTHER: Then I spoke and you heard! . . . May the one who's worthy get the worthy one, may mighty love reign, and unite the deserted hearts so that they may comfort each other!

SWANWHITE'S MOTHER: And their hearts have exchanged kisses, their souls embraced each other! May sorrow give way to joy and may Earth rejoice over their young happiness!

PRINCE'S MOTHER: May the Powers grant that!

SWANWHITE'S MOTHER: May their love be tested in the fires of suffering!

PRINCE'S MOTHER (*picks up the* PRINCE'*s helmet*): May sorrow give way to joy . . . on the morning of this day, a year after he lost his mother.

(*She substitutes white and red feathers for the black.*)

SWANWHITE'S MOTHER: Give me your hand, Sister, and may the tests begin!

PRINCE'S MOTHER: Here's my hand, and with it my son's! . . . Now we have betrothed them . . .

SWANWHITE'S MOTHER: In decency and honor!

PRINCE'S MOTHER: Now I'll go to open the Blue Tower! And then the two youngsters may fall into each other's arms . . .

SWANWHITE'S MOTHER: In decency and honor!

PRINCE'S MOTHER: And we'll meet again on the green meadow where there are no sorrows.

SWANWHITE'S MOTHER (*points at* SWANWHITE): Listen! . . . She's dreaming about him! . . . that foolish, wicked woman, who believed she could part two lovers! . . . Now they're wandering hand in hand in the land of dreams under whispering firs, under singing lindens, and they're playing and smiling . . .

PRINCE'S MOTHER: Sh-h! Morning's here, I can hear the robin singing and see the stars disappearing into the firmament. . . Farewell, Sister! (*Goes, taking her swan garment with her.*)

SWANWHITE'S MOTHER: Farewell! . . . .

She passes her hand over SWANWHITE *as if she were blessing her; then takes her swan's garment when she has closed the gate. The clock on the table strikes three times. The harp on the table becomes silent for a moment and then begins playing a delightful melody.*

SWANWHITE *wakes up, looks about, listens to the harp, gets out of bed, runs her hands over her hair, looks with pleasure at her small white feet, and notices the white garment on the bed. Then she sits down at her place by the table.*

She seems to be observing someone sitting in the PRINCE's *place; she looks into his eyes, smiles in recognition, and extends her hand. Her lips move as if she were talking, occasionally become still as if she were listening to answers.*

She points meaningfully at the helmet's red and white feathers and bends forward as if she were whispering. Then she leans back and breathes deeply as if she were breathing in a fragrance. She catches something in the air and then kisses her finger as if returning a kiss. She writes with her pen after caressing it as if it were a bird and pushes the parchment across the table. Her eyes seem to follow "his" pen when it writes the answer and then picks up the parchment which she reads and stuffs it down into her dress.

She strokes her black dress, indicating the sad change in her appearance. Then she smiles at the assumed answer and bursts into a good laugh.

She indicates that her hair is combed, gets up, steps forward, and, shyly extends her "white" foot . . . stops, waiting for a reply which she receives with embarrassment and quickly conceals her foot.

Now she goes to her chest, takes out the chess pieces, places them on the lionskin, makes a gesture of invitation, lies down, sets up the pieces, and begins a game as if with an invisible competitor.

The harp becomes silent for a moment and then takes up a new melody.

The chess game ends, and SWANWHITE *seems to be talking with the invisible competitor. Suddenly she moves away as if he were coming too close to her. With a warning gesture she jumps up, looks reproachfully at her companion, takes the white garment, and hurries to conceal herself back of the bed.*

*

The PRINCE *appears outside the gates. He tries to open them, but in vain. He "throws" a look upwards—the height of sorrow and despair.*

SWANWHITE (*forward*): Who comes with the sunrise?

PRINCE: The one you love, your prince, your everything!

SWANWHITE: From where does the one I love come?

PRINCE: From the land of dreams, from the sunrise back of the rose-colored mountains, from whispering fir, from sighing linden.

SWANWHITE: What was the one I love doing in the land of dreams, beyond the sunrise?

PRINCE: He played and smiled, he wrote her name, he played chess on a lionskin!

SWANWHITE: With whom did he play? With whom?

PRINCE: With Swanwhite!

SWANWHITE: It is he! . . . Welcome to my castle, at my table, in my arms!

PRINCE: Who will open the golden gates?

SWANWHITE: Let me take your hand! . . . It's as cold as your heart is warm.

PRINCE: My body has slept in the Blue Tower while my soul wandered in the land of dreams! . . . The tower was cold and dark!

SWANWHITE: I'll warm your hand by my bosom . . . I'll warm your hand with my eyes . . . I'll warm your hand with my kiss!

PRINCE: Let the light of your eyes shine on my darkness!

SWANWHITE: *Your* darkness?

PRINCE: Neither the sun nor the moon shine in the Blue Tower!

SWANWHITE: Rise, sun! Blow warm, wind! Roll, sea! . . .
Golden gate, you think you can keep two hearts, two
hands, two lips apart! Nothing can keep them apart!

PRINCE: Nothing!

Two doors slide from the sides in front of the gates, so that
SWANWHITE *and the* PRINCE *can not see each other.*

SWANWHITE: Alas, what word was uttered? Who heard it?
Who is punishing us?

PRINCE: I'm not parted from you, dearest, for the sound of
my voice reaches you; it goes through copper, steel, and
stone and caresses your little ear warmly; in my thoughts I
embrace you, in my dreams I kiss you, nothing will ever
keep us apart on Earth again! Nothing!

SWANWHITE: Nothing!

PRINCE: I see you even if my eye doesn't see you, I taste you,
for you throw roses into my mouth. . . .

SWANWHITE: But I want you in my arms!

PRINCE: I'm in your arms!

SWANWHITE: No, I want to feel your heart against mine . . .
I want to sleep on your arm! Oh, let us, let us! Kind God!
Let us have each other!

(*The swallows twitter; a little white feather falls down.*
SWANWHITE *picks it up and discovers it is a key. She opens the*
entrances and the gates. The PRINCE *enters.* SWANWHITE *leaps*
into his arms. The PRINCE *kisses her mouth.*)

SWANWHITE: You're not kissing me!

PRINCE: I did!

SWANWHITE: I don't feel your kisses!

PRINCE: Then you don't love me!

SWANWHITE: Hug me!

PRINCE: I'll choke you!

SWANWHITE: No, I'm breathing!

PRINCE: Give me your soul!

SWANWHITE: Here! . . . Give me yours!

PRINCE: Here! . . . Now I have yours, and you mine!

SWANWHITE: I want mine back!

PRINCE: And I mine!

SWANWHITE: Try finding it!

PRINCE: We're lost! You are I, and I am you!

SWANWHITE: We are one!

PRINCE: The good God heard your prayer! . . . We have got each other!

SWANWHITE: We have got each other, but I don't have you any more, I can't feel the touch of your hand, not the caress of your lips; I don't see your eyes, I don't hear your voice . . . you are gone.

PRINCE: I am here!

SWANWHITE: Down here; but I want to meet you up there, in the land of dreams.

PRINCE: Let's fly up there, on the wings of sleep . . .

SWANWHITE: On your arm!

PRINCE: In my arms!

SWANWHITE: In your arms!

PRINCE: This is bliss.

SWANWHITE: Eternal, endless, without a flaw!

PRINCE: Can anyone part us?

SWANWHITE: No one!

PRINCE: Are you my bride?

SWANWHITE: Are you my bridegroom?

PRINCE: In the land of dreams! Not here!

SWANWHITE: Where are we?

PRINCE: Down here!

SWANWHITE: Where the clouds move, where the sea thunders, where the earth weeps on the grass every night before the sun goes up! Where the hawk tears the dove to pieces, where the swallow kills the fly, where the leaf falls and becomes dust; where hair turns white and cheeks sink in, where eyes fade and hands wither! Down here!

PRINCE: Let's flee!

SWANWHITE: Let's flee!

*

The GARDENER *clad in green with apron and kneepants; with scissors and knife in his belt, suddenly pops up back of the table. He has a little wooden bowl in his hand and goes about sowing seeds.*

PRINCE: Who are you?

GARDENER: I sow, I sow!

PRINCE: What are you sowing?

GARDENER: Seed, seed, seed!

PRINCE: What kind?

GARDENER: Harmony and discord! One goes over here; two go over there; when the bridal gown is on, the harmony's off! I sow in discord, and you'll reap in harmony. One and one makes one, but one and one also makes three; one and one makes two, but two makes three! Do you understand all that?

PRINCE: Earthworm, dustdigger, you who go with your forehead to the ground and show your back to heaven, what do you want to teach me?

GARDENER: That you are an earthworm and a dustdigger! And because you turn your back on earth, the earth will turn its back on you! . . . Good morning! (*Sinks behind the table.*)

*

SWANWHITE: What was that? Who was it?

PRINCE: That was the green gardener.

SWANWHITE: Green? He surely was blue?

PRINCE: He was green, darling!

SWANWHITE: How can you say what isn't so?

PRINCE: My very, very dearest, I have only said what's so.

SWANWHITE: Alas, you don't say what's true.

PRINCE: Whose voice do I hear? Not my Swanwhite's!

SWANWHITE: Whom does my eye see? . . . Not my prince, whose mere name once could fascinate me as the river sprite's[6] music, as the sea virgin's[7] song on green billows. . . . Who are you? You strange man with evil eyes . . . and gray hair!

PRINCE: You saw that now for the first time. My hair turned gray in half a night in the tower because of my longing for my Swanwhite who no longer exists . . .

SWANWHITE: Yes, Swanwhite is here!

PRINCE: No, because there stands a girl in black, whose face is black . . .

SWANWHITE: Didn't you see before that I was dressed in black? . . . Then you don't love me!

PRINCE: You who are standing there, angry, mean, no! . . .

SWANWHITE: Then you were false a bit ago?

PRINCE: No, because someone else was standing here then! . . . Now . . . now you threw a nettle into my mouth!

SWANWHITE: Now your violets smell of stinkweed . . . Ugh!

PRINCE: That's the punishment for my failing my young king!

SWANWHITE: I wish I had waited for the young king!

PRINCE: Wait! He'll come!

SWANWHITE: I won't wait! I'll go to meet him!

PRINCE: Then I'll stay!

SWANWHITE (*goes toward the back*): This was love!

PRINCE (*beside himself*): Where is Swanwhite? Where, where, where? The most beautiful, the dearest, the best?

SWANWHITE: Seek her!

PRINCE: Not down here, then!

SWANWHITE: Somewhere else! (*Goes.*)

*

The PRINCE *is alone; sits down at the table, his head in his hands; weeps. A gust of wind sweeps through the room so that drapes and curtains flutter and a sighing rushes over the strings of the harp. The* PRINCE *gets up, goes toward the bed,*

and stops to observe the pillow which has the impress of
SWANWHITE'*s head in profile. He picks up the pillow and kisses*
it. A noise outside. He sits down at the table.

The doors to the rooms are opened. The three MAIDS *can be*
seen, now sullen-faced. The STEPMOTHER *enters from the back,*
also sullen-faced.

STEPMOTHER (*softly*): Good morning, good prince! How did
you sleep?

PRINCE: Where is Swanwhite?

STEPMOTHER: She has gone to her young king to celebrate
her wedding. Aren't you thinking about doing that sort of
thing soon?

PRINCE: I have only one thought . . .

STEPMOTHER: About young Swanwhite?

PRINCE: Is she too young for me?

STEPMOTHER: Gray hair usually is accompanied by common
sense . . . I have a sensible daughter . . .

PRINCE: Is my hair gray?

STEPMOTHER: He doesn't know, he doesn't believe it! Girls!
Signe, Elsa, Tova! Laugh at the young suitor with his gray
hair. (*The* GIRLS *laugh. The* STEPMOTHER *joins in.*)

PRINCE: Where is Swanwhite?

STEPMOTHER: Follow the clues! Here's one! (*Gives him a*
parchment on which something is written.)

PRINCE (*reads*): Did she write this?

STEPMOTHER: You know her handwriting, her hand! . . .
What has her hand written?

PRINCE: That she hates me, and loves someone else . . . that
she has played with me, that she spits out my kisses, and is
throwing my heart into the pig pen. . . . Now I want to
die! Now I am dead!

STEPMOTHER: A knight doesn't die because of a girl's trifling!
He shows he's a man and chooses someone else!

PRINCE: Someone else? When there's only one.

STEPMOTHER: At least two! And my Magdalena has seven tuns of gold!

PRINCE: Seven?

STEPMOTHER: More than that! (*Pause.*)

PRINCE: Where is Swanwhite?

STEPMOTHER: And Magdalena can perform many tricks . . .

PRINCE: Can she bewitch, too?

STEPMOTHER: She can certainly bewitch a little prince.

PRINCE (*observing the parchment*): Did Swanwhite write this?

STEPMOTHER: Magdalena wouldn't write anything like that!

PRINCE: Is Magdalena good?

STEPMOTHER: She's goodness itself! She doesn't trifle with sacred feelings. She doesn't avenge a little wrong, she's faithful to the one she loves.

PRINCE: Then she's beautiful!

STEPMOTHER: Not beautiful!

PRINCE: Then she isn't good! . . . Tell me more about her!

STEPMOTHER: See her!

PRINCE: Where?

STEPMOTHER: Here!

PRINCE: Has Swanwhite written this? . . .

STEPMOTHER: Magdalena would have written affectionately.

PRINCE: What would she have written?

STEPMOTHER: That . . .

PRINCE: Say the word! Say *love,* if you can!

STEPMOTHER: Lobe!

PRINCE: You can't say the word!

STEPMOTHER: Lubbe!

PRINCE: No!

STEPMOTHER: Magdalena can say it! May she come?

PRINCE: She may come!

*

STEPMOTHER (*gets up. Speaks to the* MAIDS): Cover the prince's eyes so he may take in his arms a princess, the like of whom isn't to be found in seven kingdoms!

(SIGNE *comes forward, puts a blindfold over the* PRINCE's *eyes.*)

STEPMOTHER (*strikes her hands together*): Well? Isn't she coming? (*The peacock clatters, the doves coo.*) Has my magic failed me? Or what? . . . Where is the bride?

Four GIRLS *carrying baskets of white and pink roses enter from the back; music can be heard from above. The* GIRLS *go up to the bed and strew roses on it.*

Then two KNIGHTS *with lowered viziers enter. They take the* PRINCE *by the hand and conduct him toward the back where they are met by the supposed* MAGDALENA *conducted by two* LADIES. *The bride is heavily veiled.*

The STEPMOTHER *signals to everyone but the bridal couple to go and then goes out herself after she has drawn the drapes and closed the gates.*

PRINCE: Is my bride here?

FALSE MAGDALENA: Who is your bride?

PRINCE: I don't remember her name! Who is your bridegroom?

FALSE MAGDALENA: The one whose name may not be spoken!

PRINCE: Say it if you can!

FALSE MAGDALENA: I can, but I don't want to!

PRINCE: Say it if you can!

FALSE MAGDALENA: Say mine first!

PRINCE: Seven tuns of gold, a crooked back, mean, harelipped! What is my name? Say it if you can!

FALSE MAGDALENA: Prince Grayhairs!

PRINCE: That's right! (*The "false" Magdalena throws off her veil.*) SWANWHITE *stands revealed in her white gown with a wreath of roses in her hair.* Who am I now?

PRINCE: You are a rose!

SWANWHITE: You are a violet!

PRINCE (*takes off his blindfold*): You are Swanwhite!

SWANWHITE: And you . . . are . . .

PRINCE: Sh-h!

SWANWHITE: You are mine!

PRINCE: But you went away, away from my kisses . . .

SWANWHITE: And came back! For I love you!

PRINCE: And you wrote evil words . . .

SWANWHITE: That I have erased, for I love you!

PRINCE: And you said I was false!

SWANWHITE: What does it matter when you're faithful and I love you?

PRINCE: And you wanted to go to the young king?

SWANWHITE: But went to you, because I love you!

PRINCE: Now tell me all your complaints.

SWANWHITE: No, for I've forgotten them, for I love you!

PRINCE: If you love me, are you my bride?

SWANWHITE: Yes, yes!

PRINCE: May Heaven bless our union then!

SWANWHITE: In the land of dreams!

PRINCE: On my arm!

Leads SWANWHITE *to the bed, puts his sword in the middle*[8] *and* SWANWHITE *on one side of it, himself on the other. Golden clouds become rose-colored, the rose trees sigh; the harp plays delightful music.*

PRINCE: Good night, my queen!

SWANWHITE: Good morning, beloved! . . . I hear your heart beat, I hear your heart sigh like the billows of the sea, like the trot of the steed, like the wing of the eagle. . . . Hold me by the hand!

PRINCE: Here! Now we'll lift our wings. . . .

*

STEPMOTHER (*enters with the three* MAIDS *who are carrying torches. All four are gray-haired*): I must see my work completed before the duke comes. Magdalena, my daughter, betrothed to the prince . . . while Swanwhite's confined in the tower. . . . (*Goes up to the bed.*) They're already sleeping in each other's arms. Girls, be my witnesses! . . . (*The* MAIDS *approach the bed.*) What do I see? Why, you're gray-haired!

SIGNE: And you, too, Your Grace!

STEPMOTHER: I? Let me see! (ELSA *holds up a mirror.*) The work of evil powers! . . . Maybe the prince has got his black hair back? . . . Hold the light over here! (*The* GIRLS *shine their lights on the sleepers.*) By God, it's true! . . . Yet! It is beautiful! . . . But the sword! Who has placed the sword so the betrothal isn't valid?

   She tries to take away the sword, but the PRINCE *holds onto it without waking up.*

SIGNE: Your Grace, this is witchcraft!

STEPMOTHER: How so?

SIGNE: This is not Lady Magdalena!

STEPMOTHER: Who is it? Help my eyes!

SIGNE: See, it's Lady Swanwhite!

STEPMOTHER: Swanwhite? . . . Is this the devil's work or have I done what I didn't want to do? . . .

   (*The* PRINCE *turns and stops with his lips on* SWANWHITE'S.)

STEPMOTHER (*gripped by the beautiful sight*): I never saw anything more beautiful! . . . Two roses meeting in the wind; two stars falling from the firmament and meeting in their fall; no, it's all too beautiful! Youth, beauty, innocence, love! . . . Memories, delightful memories when I lived in my father's home, when *he* loved me, the young man I never got . . . What did I say he did to me?

SIGNE: Your Grace said he loved!

STEPMOTHER: Then I said the great word right! Loved! That's what he called me: "beloved," before he went to war. . . . (*Lost in thought.*)

He never came back! . . . So I had to marry the one I couldn't stand! . . . Now my life's over; and I'll have to rejoice over happiness I never had! I will rejoice . . . over others' happiness . . . still some kind of love! . . . But my Magdalena? Will she rejoice? Almighty love, eternal creative God, how You have turned my lionheart soft! Where is my strength, where is my hate? Where is my vengeance! (*She sits down and observes the sleepers.*) I remember a song, a love song which *he* sang in my youth, that last evening . . . (*Gets up, wakes up as if from a dream and becomes furious. Growls.*) People, this way! Come, steward, bailiff, executioner, all of you! (*She jerks the sword out of the bed and throws it out toward the back.*) People, this way!

*

Noise; the SERVANTS *dash in.*

*

STEPMOTHER: Take a look! The prince, the young king's vassal, has despoiled his lord's bride! Be witnesses to the ugly deed! May the traitor be brought in chains and iron to his lord, and may the harlot be put in the Iron Virgin! (*The* PRINCE *and* SWANWHITE *wake up.*) Bailiff and executioner, seize the prince! (*They do.*)

PRINCE: Where's my sword! I'll use it not against evil, but for innocence!

STEPMOTHER: Whose innocence?

PRINCE: My bride's!

STEPMOTHER: The harlot's innocence! Prove it!

SWANWHITE: Mother, Mother! (*The white swan flies past outside.*)

STEPMOTHER: Give me a pair of scissors, girls! I'll clip the harlot's hair![9] (SIGNE *hands her scissors. The* STEPMOTHER *grabs* SWANWHITE *by the hair, but the scissors open and cannot be closed.*) Now I'll clip your beauty and your love! (*Then*

panic seizes her and spreads to the MAIDS *and the* SERVANTS.)
Is the enemy upon us? Why do you tremble? . . .

SIGNE: Your Grace! The dogs are barking, the horses neighing—that means strangers are coming!

STEPMOTHER: Quickly, everyone to the drawbridge! Everyone! To the walls! Fire, water, swords, broadaxes!

[CURTAIN]

ACT III

The three MAIDS *are standing very busy in their rooms:* SIGNE, *the false attendant in the Pewter Room;* ELSA, *the tiny one in the Clothes Room;* TOVA, *the ugly and the faithful one in the Fruit Room.*

GARDENER (*enters*): Signe, my daughter, help me.

SIGNE: Tell me first who it was that made all that noise when he came? Was it our lord, the duke, returning from war?

GARDENER: No, it wasn't the duke; it was a messenger from the young king, Lady Swanwhite's bridegroom—with a large armed following! Misfortune's upon us, there'll be war . . . and the castle will be burned down!

SIGNE: Your seeds have sprouted, your seeds of dissension; reap as you have sowed . . .

GARDENER: False Signe, you were the one who betrayed us when you fetched the duchess Stand-by, the horn that could have saved us . . .

SIGNE: A faithful servant should be false toward her master's enemies . . .

GARDENER: But the castle will be razed if the duke doesn't come. How shall we get the duke to come?

SIGNE: If there's time, there's a way! First, the banquet! I'm cleaning the pewter, Elsa's brushing the clothes, Tova drying the fruit . . . But isn't the young king along?

GARDENER: Only the ambassadors and their following . . .

SIGNE: Where's the young king?

GARDENER: Who knows? Maybe he's along but disguised . . .

SIGNE: And the prince?

GARDENER: In the tower!—Why did you hate him?

SIGNE: I? I didn't hate him . . . No, no, no!

GARDENER: You probably . . .

SIGNE: Don't say any more . . .

GARDENER: Should you hate the one you love?

SIGNE: Yes, when you don't get him . . .

GARDENER: When you don't get him? But Lady Swanwhite'll not get her prince, and she loves him in death, beyond death . . .

SIGNE: Is the prince going to die?

GARDENER: You know that!

SIGNE: No, by all that's sacred! But he mustn't die . . . Save him!

GARDENER: How?

SIGNE: Through the secret passage—here's the entrance—you know, here in the floor . . .

GARDENER: The duchess will flood the passage!

SIGNE: That may be. . . . But save the prince! Save him, quickly! And then into the boat and out to sea!

GARDENER: Well, I'll go to make amends for the wrong I've done; if I don't come back, then I'll have done penance . . .

SIGNE: God protect you on your journey . . .

SWANWHITE (*enters from the back*): What wickedness are you up to here?

GARDENER (*on his knees*): I'm here to make amends for the evil I've done . . .

SWANWHITE: How can you? You sowed seeds of dissension. What are you sowing now?

GARDENER (*strewing seeds about*): I'm sowing unity, happiness, peace, for the good of all, to the harm of no one!—Don't judge me, milady, for I'm not to blame for your quarrel!

SWANWHITE: Quarrel? Whether you were blue or green?

GARDENER: Yes! Look at me now with both of your beautiful eyes at once . . .

SWANWHITE: I am looking!

GARDENER (*turns*): See then that I'm blue on one side, green on the other!

SWANWHITE: So you're both! You old scamp, who have taught me wisdom! Thank you!—But where are you going now?

GARDENER: To fetch the prince!

SWANWHITE: You? Can bad become good?

GARDENER: Not always!—Now I'll go through the secret passage; either I'll come back with him, or I'll stay there—without him!

SWANWHITE: May God bless you and keep you! (*The* GARDENER *goes down through the opening in the floor.*)

*

SWANWHITE (*to* SIGNE): Are you betraying your father?

SIGNE: No! Not my father!

SWANWHITE: But the prince?

SIGNE: Not the prince!

SWANWHITE: Me then?

(SIGNE *does not answer.*)

SWANWHITE: Me then?

SIGNE: Milady! Misfortune's upon all of us; only one can save us—your father, the duke.

SWANWHITE: Yes, the duke, my glorious father! But he can't hear us in our need, since you betrayed me and handed the horn to the duchess.

SIGNE: Do you know where she has hidden it?

SWANWHITE: I'll have to think! (*She considers.*)

SIGNE: Where?

SWANWHITE: Sh-h!————I can see it . . . back of the mirror in her . . . in her silver room!

SIGNE: Then I'll go get it!

SWANWHITE: You? for my sake?

SIGNE: Don't thank me! Misfortune's upon all of us! No, no thanks!

SWANWHITE: You're not betraying us?

SIGNE: Us? Not all, no one and any one, one and one, if I only knew! One loves the one one hates, but not always! The one one hates, one doesn't love, not always! I'm torn apart, worn out; we'll see Stand-by; I'll stand by but will not stand by; perhaps! (*Goes.*)

SWANWHITE: Riddles and puzzles!—Elsa, Tova, come! (*They come in.*) Over here! They're listening to us! Beautiful Elsa, good Tova, stand by my side; I fear something I don't know; someone's coming—I don't know who; I can hear it in my heart, see it in my breast—a danger; a breath as cold as ice is blowing on me, a crude hand is touching my young, tiny breasts as the hawk touches the dove's young ones. . . . Alas, it's wild game, cabbage and onions, everything that reeks, goat's beard and nettles. . . . Now he's here!—The young king!

*

The young KING *enters from in back, lusty and somewhat intoxicated.* ELSA *and* TOVA *stand in front of* SWANWHITE.

KING (*scans the three insolently*): Three of you!—Do you know
    who I am?

ELSA: The knight Winebag!

KING: Cheeky! Come and I'll kiss you!—for you are tiny,
    beautiful, and mean! (*To* TOVA) You are ugly and good!
    Tell me where Princess Swanwhite is.

ELSA: Guess!

KING: You?—Oh well . . . but you have red hands!—so
    you're no princess!—Do you know my name?

ELSA: Count Buck!

KING: I like mean girls, you little goat, come into my arms!

ELSA: Right now?

KING: Imagine if the princess heard us!

TOVA: She doesn't hear such things, she has an ear only for
    the song of the nightingale, for the music of the linden, for
    the sighing of the wind above the billows . . .

KING: Don't be so long-winded, you ugly thing; you say too
    much at a time. . . . Mind your manners, maids, and tell
    where the princess is, otherwise, by Satan, Stepmother's
    steel whip will rain down on those backs of yours. Where is
    Princess Swanwhite?

SWANWHITE (*steps forward*): Here she is!

KING (*looks her over*): You? (*Pause.*) I can't believe it! Why, I
    saw her portrait, and it was beautiful, but I suppose that
    faithless prince had painted it to flatter me!—Why, you
    don't have a nose, child; and rolls of fat by your eyes; your
    lips are too thick. . . . Now I ask: Is this Swanwhite?

SWANWHITE: It's I!

KING (*sits down*): So this is . . . all!—Can you dance? play
    chess? paint? sing? (*Pause.*) Nothing!—and for this nothing
    I was ready to storm the castle, burn it, sack it, wage war.
    (*Pause.*) Can't you at least talk? Talk away a long
    evening?—Not that either!

SWANWHITE (*dully*): I can talk, but not with you!

KING: You sound like a chimneysweep. . . . Maybe you're deaf?

SWANWHITE: Certain voices do not reach my ear.

KING: And blind, and lame! (*Pause.*) Frankly, too much effort for such a little gain!—(*Pause.*) Go in peace! or let me go. . . . Prince Faithless may pluck his geese with the injured party! (*Gets up.*) And with me! (*Goes.*)

SWANWHITE, ELSA, *and* TOVA *raise their hands and remain standing like that. The harp plays.*

*

The PRINCE *comes up from the secret passage.* SWANWHITE *leaps into his arms. The harp plays.* ELSA *and* TOVA *go out at the back. The* PRINCE *and* SWANWHITE *try to talk but cannot. The* KING *now appears in the Clothes Room spying and listening.*

SWANWHITE: Is this good-bye?

PRINCE: Don't say that!

SWANWHITE: He's here, has been here, the king! Your king!

PRINCE: Then it's good-bye, forever!

SWANWHITE: No, he didn't see me, he didn't hear me, he didn't like me . . .

PRINCE: But he'll try to kill me . . .

SWANWHITE: All of them will . . . Where are you going?

PRINCE: To the beach . . .

SWANWHITE: Out to sea, in storm and current, dear heart, my joy . . .

PRINCE: I'll drink to my wedding in the billows . . .

SWANWHITE: Then I'll die!

PRINCE: Then we'll meet! never to part, never again!

SWANWHITE: Never again! But if I don't, I'll mourn you out of the grave . . .

PRINCE: For every tear from your eyes, my coffin will fill with blood, but every time you're happy on earth, my coffin will fill with rose petals!

SWANWHITE: It's getting dark!

PRINCE: I walk in light, in your light, for I love . . .

SWANWHITE: Take my soul, take my life.

PRINCE: I have—take mine!—You have them!—Now my body goes, but my soul will stay . . .

SWANWHITE: Here is my body, but my soul goes—with you!

(*The* PRINCE *and* SWANWHITE *try to talk but only their lips move. The* PRINCE *goes down into the secret passage.*)

The KING *has observed the scene, and has been moved by his "discovery" of* SWANWHITE. *He has been ashamed at first, then overcome with admiration and fascination; when the* PRINCE *has gone, he rushes forward and falls to his knees.*

KING: Swanwhite, beautiful creation of God, fear nothing, for now I have seen you, most perfect of women, now I have heard your voice of silver strings, but it was with *his* eyes I saw and with his ears I heard; I never may myself, for I don't have your love; I see in your eyes that you do not see me, and you don't hear my words; you exist only for him, and if I got you, I'd be holding a corpse in my arms; forgive me for what I have done, forget I ever existed and never think I'd dare to touch you with an impure thought; your memory alone shall pursue me and punish me, but give me your voice in parting so I may keep its echo in my heart. . . . One word! Any word, a resounding one, only one! (*Pause.*)

SWANWHITE (*harshly*): Go!

KING (*jumps up*): Raven! Now I answer: blood! (*Draws his sword.*) And no one else shall possess you, only I! But I want the raven, I love what is strong, hard, coarse! The dove isn't my bird!

SWANWHITE (*has retreated back of the table*): Help, Father! Stand-by, come, come, come!

KING (*cooling down*): There it came! The silver voice, the bell calling for prayer on some saint's day! Now my power's gone . . .

SWANWHITE (*half-singing*): Come, come, come!

KING: How lovely your voice is. My sword weeps and is ashamed—go hide yourself! (*Sheaths his sword*) Not the sword! But fire, set fire to the castle, death to the traitor . . . Who's there?

*

TOVA (*enters with the horn*): Here, here!

SWANWHITE: You? Not Signe?

TOVA: I took it from Signe! That eternally faithless one!

SWANWHITE *blows in the horn. A horn answers in the distance.*

KING (*panic-stricken*): Up into the saddles! Loose the reins! Press the spurs! Full speed! (*Flees through the back left.*)

(SWANWHITE *blows again. A horn just outside answers.*)

TOVA: He's coming! The glorious hero! He's coming! (*Pause.*)

(SWANWHITE *blows again.*)

DUKE (*enters.* TOVA *leaves*): Dearest, what's this about?

SWANWHITE: Father, it's about your child. . . . Look at the Iron Virgin there!

DUKE: What have you done wrong?

SWANWHITE: I discovered the prince's name in ways only love teaches; I said it . . . and I loved him.

DUKE: That's not a mortal sin! What else?

SWANWHITE: I slept by his side with the sword between us . . .

DUKE: That's still not mortal, but it wasn't sensible. . . . What else?

SWANWHITE: Nothing else!

DUKE (*calls the* EXECUTIONER): Roll out the Iron Virgin! Well, my child, where's the prince?

SWANWHITE: He's sailing home!

DUKE: Now? In this storm? . . . Alone?

SWANWHITE: Alone! What's going to happen?

DUKE: That's in the hands of God!

SWANWHITE: Is he in danger?

DUKE: A daring man's sometimes lucky . . .

SWANWHITE: He deserves to be!

DUKE: If he's innocent, he will be! . . .

SWANWHITE: He is! More than I!

*

STEPMOTHER (*enters*): How did you get here?

DUKE: By the shortest way! I wish I had come before!

STEPMOTHER: If you had come before, your child wouldn't be in misfortune!

DUKE: What misfortune?

STEPMOTHER: The one that can't be repaired!

DUKE: Do you have proof?

STEPMOTHER: Valid witnesses!

DUKE: Call the steward!

STEPMOTHER: He doesn't know about it!

DUKE (*shakes his sword*): Call the steward!

> The STEPMOTHER *trembles. Strikes her hands four times.*
> (*The* STEWARD *enters.*)

DUKE: You're to make a pie of wild game, well-spiced with onion, parsley, fennel, and fungus!

> The STEWARD *looks toward the* STEPMOTHER.

DUKE: What are you squinting for? . . . Right now! (*The* STEWARD *goes. The* DUKE *to the* STEPMOTHER.) Call the herb gardener!

STEPMOTHER: He doesn't know about it!

DUKE: And isn't going to! But he is to come! Call him! (*The* STEPMOTHER *strikes her hands six times.*)

*

(*The* HERB GARDENER *enters.*)

DUKE: Get me three lilies; a white, a red, a blue one! (*The* HERB GARDENER *glances toward the* STEPMOTHER.)

DUKE: Watch out for your head! (*The* HERB GARDENER *goes.*)

＊

DUKE: Call the witnesses! (*The* STEPMOTHER *strikes her hands once.*)

(SIGNE *enters.*)

DUKE: Testify! But in courteous words! . . . What have you seen?

SIGNE: I have seen Lady Swanwhite and the prince in one bed!

DUKE: With the sword?

SIGNE: Without!

SWANWHITE: Signe, Signe, you're testifying falsely against me, me who saved your neck from the steel whip . . . you hurt me so! And you betrayed me that night. . . . Why do you do this to me?

SIGNE: I didn't know what I was doing; I did what I didn't want to do; I did what someone else wanted; and now I don't want to live any longer; forgive me for the sake of Our Savior. . . .

SWANWHITE: I forgive you; forgive yourself, too; for you are without guilt when that evil will captured you . . .

SIGNE: But punish me first!

SWANWHITE: Aren't you punished enough when you've repented? . . .

DUKE: I don't believe it! . . . More witnesses!

＊

(*The two* KNIGHTS *enter.*)

DUKE: Are you the knights who escorted the bride? . . . Testify!

KNIGHT I: I escorted Lady Magdalena to bed!

KNIGHT II: I escorted Lady Magdalena to bed!

DUKE: What is this? A trick that has backfired! . . . More witnesses!

    (ELSA *enters.*)

DUKE: Testify!

ELSA: By the just and punishing God, I have seen Lady Swanwhite and the prince, fully dressed and with the sword between them.

DUKE: One for and one against; two not to the point! . . . I'll leave it to God's judgment! . . . Let the flower test be made!

*

TOVA (*comes forward*): Gracious lord, stern knight?

DUKE: What do you know?

TOVA: That my gracious lady is innocent!

DUKE: Child, child, you know. But teach us to know it!

TOVA: When I say what is true!

DUKE: No one believes you, but when Signe says what isn't true, they have to believe that! . . . What does Swanwhite herself say? Doesn't her pure forehead, her clear glances, her innocent mouth say that they've slandered her! Doesn't my father's eye say: That's true! . . . Well, let the almighty God pronounce judgment so that people may believe!

    The HERB GARDENER *enters with the three lilies in a vase. The* DUKE *puts the flowers in a half circle on the table. The* STEWARD *comes in with a steaming pie on a plate.*

DUKE (*places the plate so that the flowers surround it*): Whose is the white lily?

ALL (*except* SWANWHITE *and the* STEPMOTHER): Swanwhite's!

DUKE: Whose is the red lily?

ALL (*except* SWANWHITE *and the* STEPMOTHER): The prince's!

DUKE: Whose is the blue?

ALL (*except* SWANWHITE *and the* STEPMOTHER): The young king's!

DUKE: Fine! . . . Tova, my child, you who believe in innocence because you are innocent yourself! Interpret for us God's judgment and tell us the lovely secrets of the flowers! What do you see?

TOVA: I can't say the bad!

DUKE: I will, then you may say the good! . . . By the vapors of the lusty wild game's blood, by the vapors of the herbs of sensual pleasures . . . what happens?

TOVA (*observes the three lilies, which behave as her words indicate*): The white lily is closing to protect itself from impure influences. That is Swanwhite's!

ALL: Swanwhite is innocent!

TOVA: And the red one, the prince's, is closing . . . but the blue one, the king's, opens wide to breathe in sensuality!

DUKE: Correctly interpreted! What else do you see?

TOVA: I see the red lily bow respectfully in love before the white one, but the blue one twists and turns in anger and envy!

DUKE: Beautifully interpreted! . . . Who then is to have Swanwhite?

TOVA: The prince since his desires are purest and therefore strongest.

ALL (*except* SWANWHITE *and the* STEPMOTHER): The prince shall have Swanwhite!

SWANWHITE (*leaps into the* DUKE's *arms*): Oh, Father!

DUKE: Call the prince back! Blow in lures[10] and horns! Put out all the sailboats from the beach! But first! Who's to sit in the Iron Virgin? (ALL *are silent.*) Then I'll tell you! . . . The duchess, that great liar, that witch! . . . You see, you evil woman, your arts controlled everything but not love! . . . Go, and go quickly!

(STEPMOTHER *makes a gesture with her hand which seems to deafen the* DUKE.)

DUKE (*draws his sword and directs its point at the* STEPMOTHER *while he carries* SWANWHITE *on his left shoulder*): Huh, you filthy creature! My steel point pierces your arts![11]

(*The* STEPMOTHER *withdraws backward with her legs dragging, pantherwise.*)

DUKE: Now to the prince!

(*The* STEPMOTHER *stops as if turned to stone out on the balcony: opens her mouth as if she were spraying poison; the peacock and the doves fall down dead. The* STEPMOTHER *now begins to swell, her clothes are blown up and finally conceal the upper part of her body and head. The cloth in her garb is flame-colored with a pattern of snakes—and branches. The sun begins to go up. Now the ceiling slowly sinks down; smoke and fire are emitted from the hearth.*)

DUKE (*extends the cross-shaped handle of his sword toward the* STEPMOTHER): Call upon Jesus, Our Savior!

ALL: Christ, have mercy!

(*The ceiling rises; smoke and fire no longer are emitted from the hearth.*)

*

Noise outside; a murmur of voices.

*

DUKE: What now?

SWANWHITE: I know! . . . I can see it! I can hear how the water drips from his hair, I can hear that his heart has stopped, I can hear that he is no longer breathing . . . I see he is dead!

DUKE: Where do you see? Whom?

SWANWHITE: Where? . . . I see it!

DUKE: I see nothing!

SWANWHITE: May they come quickly, for they must come!

*

Four small girls carrying baskets filled with white lilies and chopped yew branches enter and strew them on the floor; four small boys with differently toned silver bells which they ring; then a priest with the crucifix; then the golden bier on which the PRINCE *is lying under a white linen cloth strewn with red and white roses. His hair is now dark again and his face young, ruddy, and radiantly handsome with a smile on his lips.*

The harp plays; the sun rises. The STEPMOTHER's *witch "shape" bursts and she stands there in her normal form.*

The bier is lowered, lighted by the rising sun.

SWANWHITE *first kneels beside the bier and kisses the* PRINCE's *face.*

ALL *weep, their hands to their eyes.*

DUKE: Fisherman, tell us the brief tale . . .

FISHERMAN: Isn't it obvious, Your Grace? . . . The young prince was already across the sound, when gripped by violent longing for the woman he loved, he decided to swim back, directly against the tide, the waves, and the wind. Then his boat didn't want to be steered any longer.

I saw his young head above the billows, I heard him call her name; and then . . . his body was gently put down on the white sand. His hair was gray from the night in the Blue Tower; his cheeks were withered from sorrow and distress, and his dry lips didn't manage a smile.

In death he lay there, young and handsome again; his dark hair wreathed his ruddy cheeks . . . and the corpse was smiling . . . see, it is still smiling! And people had gathered down on the sands, overcome by the exquisite sight said to each other: See, that is love!

SWANWHITE (*lies down beside the* PRINCE's *body*): He is dead, his heart is not singing any more, his eyes are not shining on my life, he doesn't breathe any more on me! He is smiling, but not at me; he's smiling toward heaven. I shall go with him on his journey!

DUKE: Don't kiss the dead man's lips; that's poison!

SWANWHITE: A wonderful poison if it gives me death, the death that is life for me.

DUKE: They say, my child, that the dead do not meet each other of their own will; and that what one has loved in life here does not have value there.

SWANWHITE: And love? Can't that reach beyond death?

DUKE: Wise men have denied that!

SWANWHITE: Then may he come back, down here again. God send him back from your heaven!

DUKE: A prayer in vain!

SWANWHITE: I can't pray, for, alas, the evil eye still reigns here!

DUKE: You mean the troll who burst in the sun![12] Let her be burned at the stake, alive, right now!

SWANWHITE: Burned alive. No, no; let her go her way.

DUKE: She shall be burned alive. People, raise the bonfire on the beach, so her ashes may be scattered by the wind!

SWANWHITE (*on her knees before the* DUKE): Oh no, I plead for her, my executioner: mercy!

*

STEPMOTHER (*enters, changed, released from her enchantment*): Mercy! Who said that sacred word? Who uttered that loving plea for me?

SWANWHITE: I did . . . your daughter, Mother!

STEPMOTHER: Oh God in heaven, she called me mother! . . . Who taught you?

SWANWHITE: Love!

STEPMOTHER: Blessed be love! that performs such miracles. . . . Well, my child, then it can summon the dead from the kingdom of dark death! . . . I can't do it, for love was denied to me! but you can!

SWANWHITE: What can I, poor soul do?

STEPMOTHER: You can love, you can forgive. . . . Well

then, you can do everything! . . . Learn from me, who
no longer can do anything. Go, call on his heart! And with
the help of the Almighty . . . but only with His
help . . . your beloved will hear you . . . if you can
believe!

SWANWHITE: I believe, I will, I pray!

(*Goes up to the* PRINCE'*s bier, puts one hand on his heart, the
other she holds upward. Then she bends down whispering in
the* PRINCE'*s ear three repeated times. The third time the*
PRINCE *awakens.* SWANWHITE *embraces him.* ALL *the others
kneel as if they were thanking and praising {God}. Music.*)

[CURTAIN]

Notes on 'Swanwhite'

1. The betrothal was basically a contract for the marriage of the youngsters drawn up by adult representatives.

2. An ancient poetic metaphor.

3. Argus was a legendary monster who had a human body and a hundred eyes, some of which were always awake. According to the story, Argus' eyes were used to embellish the peacock's tail.

4. The Iron Maiden was an instrument of torture shaped "in human form hinged to admit a victim, who, as the frame closed, was impaled on the spikes which stud its interior" (Webster's International Dictionary).

5. The *svanhamn* (swan's cloak) is the magic garment which, according to Scandinavian mythology, permitted the wearer to get about easily and swiftly, generally without danger of exposure of identity.

6. See p. 157, n. 8.

7. According to Swedish folklore, the Sea Virgin lives in large beautiful halls; when the River Sprite plays his violin, she sings and little white-clad childlike figures rise from the waves and dance in a circle on the shore.

8. Reminiscent of the old European (and early American) custom of bundling, lying in the same bed without being undressed with a board between the boy and the girl—during courtship.

9. An old means of punishing an adulteress by identifying her conspicuously.

10. See p. 157, n. 2.

11. See p. 159, n. 24.

12. Swedish folklore is rich in tales about trolls, the "supernatural" and generally evil creatures of the human imagination.

Bibliographic
Notes

THE SWEDISH EDITIONS of Strindberg's works are John Landquist's *Strindbergs samlade skrifter* (55 vols.; Stockholm: Bonnier, 1912–20); G. Carlheim-Gyllensköld's supplementary *Samlade otryckta skrifter* (2 vols.; Stockholm: Bonnier, 1918–19), and Carl Reinhold Smedmark's ongoing *August Strindbergs Dramer* (Stockholm: Bonnier, 1962—).

The Swedish bibliographies are in E. N. Tigerstedt's *Svensk litteraturhistoria* (Stockholm: Bonnier, 1948 and later printings) and the annual bibliography in the journal *Samlaren*. The basic American bibliographies are Esther H. Rapp's bibliography of Strindberg in England and America (*Scandinavian Studies* 23 (1950): 1–22, 49–59, 100–37), A. Gustafson's bibliography in his *A History of Swedish Literature* (Minneapolis: University of Minnesota Press, 1961 and later printings), and the annual bibliographies in *Scandinavian Studies* and the *Publications of the Modern Language Association*.

For a list of the most useful primary and secondary sources in English see the bibliography on pages 207–15 of my *August Strindberg* (Boston: Twayne, 1976). For those who do not read Swedish, the indispensable primary sources are Strindberg's *Open Letters to the Intimate Theater* (Seattle: University of Washington Press, 1967), my translation of the Damascus trilogy (University of Washington Press, 1979), and available translations of such other autobiographical works as *The Son of a Servant, A Madman's Defense* (Garden

City: Doubleday, 1967), and *Inferno, Alone and Other Writings* (Garden City: Doubleday, 1968), *From an Occult Diary: Marriage with Harriet Bosse* (New York: Hill and Wang, 1965), and *Letters of Strindberg to Harriet Bosse* (New York: Nelson, 1959).